STRATEGIC CONTROL SYSTEMS

THE WEST SERIES IN STRATEGIC MANAGEMENT

Consulting Editor
Charles W. Hofer

Setting Strategic Goals and Objectives, 2d ed.
Max D. Richards

Strategy Formulation: Issues and Concepts
Charles W. Hofer

Strategy Formulation: Power and Politics, 2d ed.
Ian C. MacMillan and Patricia E. Jones

Strategy Implementation: Structure, Systems, and Process, 2d ed.
Jay R. Galbraith and Robert K. Kazanjian

Strategic Control
Peter Lorange, Michael F. Scott Morton, and Sumantra Ghoshal

Macroenvironmental Analysis for Strategic Management
Liam Fahey and V. K. Narayanan

STRATEGIC CONTROL SYSTEMS

Peter Lorange

WHARTON SCHOOL
UNIVERSITY OF PENNSYLVANIA

Michael F. Scott Morton

MASSACHUSETTS INSTITUTE OF TECHNOLOGY

Sumantra Ghoshal

INSEAD

WEST PUBLISHING COMPANY
St. Paul   New York   Los Angeles   San Francisco

Acknowledgment: The excerpt on page 94 is from James Brian Quinn STRATEGIES FOR CHANGE—LOGICAL INCREMENTALISM © Richard D. Irwin, Inc. 1980. Reprinted with permission.

Copyediting by Joan Torkildson

Interior art by Alice B. Thiede, Carto-Graphics

Cover design by Peter Thiel, Kim Rafferty

Typesetting by Huron Valley Graphics, Inc. Typefaces are Aster and Optima.

Index prepared by Lois Oster

Library of Congress Cataloging-in-Publication Data

Lorange, Peter.
  Strategic control,

  (West series in strategic management)
  Bibliography: p.
  Includes index.
  1. Strategic planning. I. Scott Morton, Michael F.
II. Ghoshal, Sumantra. III. Title. IV. Series.
HD30.28.L673 1986   658.4'012   86-1315
ISBN 0-314-85258-1

To our fathers:

Per Lorange, William Scott Morton, Basanta Ghoshal

CONTENTS

4

Classical Views of Strategic Control: Controlling the Strategic Momentum   *62*

5

Understanding Discontinuity: Strategic Control   *100*

6

Strategic Control and Diversification: Managing Scope and Consistency   *124*

7

Operationalizing Strategic Control   *137*

8

Information Technology and Strategic Control   *150*

9

Issues for the Future   *166*

FOREWORD

This series is a response to the rapid and significant changes that have occurred in the strategic management/business policy area over the past twenty-five years. Although strategic management/business policy is a subject of long standing in management schools, it was traditionally viewed as a capstone course whose primary purpose was to *integrate* the knowledge and skills students had gained in the functional disciplines. During the past fifteen years, however, strategic management/business policy has developed a substantive content of its own. Originally, this content focused on the concepts of corporate and business strategies and on the processes by which such strategies were formulated and implemented within organizations. More recently, as Figure 1 and Table 1 illustrate, the scope of the field has broadened to include the study of both the functions and responsibilities of top management and the organizational systems and processes used to establish overall organizational goals and objectives and to formulate, implement, and control the strategies and policies necessary to achieve these goals and objectives.

When the *West Series in Business Policy and Planning* was originally published, most of the texts in the field did not yet reflect this extension in scope. The principal purpose of the original series was, therefore, to fill this void by incorporating the latest research findings and conceptual thought in the field into each of the texts in the series. In the intervening seven years, the series has succeeded to a far greater degree than we could have ever hoped.

However, the pace of research in strategic management/business policy has, if anything, increased since the publication of the original series. Some changes are, thus, clearly in order. It is the purpose of the *West Series in Strategic Management* to continue the tradition

Figure 1   The Evolution of
Business Policy/Strategic Management as a Field of Study

The Traditional Boundary of Business Policy

The Current Boundaries of Strategic Management

Some Major Contributors to the Redefinition of the Field

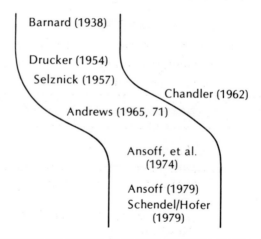

of innovative, state-of-the-art coverage of the field of strategic management started by the *West Series in Business Policy and Planning* both through revisions to all the books in the original series, and through the addition of two new titles. In making such revisions, care has been taken to ensure not only that the various texts fit together as a series, but also that each is self-contained and addresses a major topic in the field. In addition, the series has been designed so that it covers almost all the major topics that form the

Table 1   The Major Subfields of Business Policy/Strategic Management

    1. Boards of Directors

    2. The Nature of General Management Work

    3. Middle-Level General Management

*   4. Stakeholder Analysis

    5. Organizational Goal Formulation

    6. Corporate Social Policy and Management Ethics

*   7. Macroenvironmental Analysis

*   8. Strategy Formulation and Strategic Decision Making

    9. Corporate-Level Strategy (including Mergers, Acquisitions, and Divestitures)

   10. Business-Level Strategy

* 11. Strategic Planning and Information Systems

   12. The Strategy-Structure-Performance Linkage

   13. The Design of Macroorganizational Structure and Systems

✔ 14. Strategic Control Systems

* 15. Organizational Culture

   16. Leadership Style for General Managers

   17. The Strategic Management of Small Businesses and New Ventures

   18. The Strategic Management of High Tech Organizations

   19. The Strategic Management of Not-for-Profit Organizations

✔ Indicates subfields that are covered extensively by this text

* Indicates other subfields that are discussed in this text

heartland of strategic management, as Figure 2 illustrates. The individual texts in the series are

Setting Strategic Goals and Objectives, 2d ed.
Max D. Richards

Strategy Formulation: Issues and Concepts
Charles W. Hofer

Strategy Formulation: Power and Politics, 2d ed.
Ian C. MacMillan and Patricia E. Jones

Strategy Implementation: Structure, Systems, and Process, 2d ed.
Jay R. Galbraith and Robert K. Kazanjian

Strategic Control
Peter Lorange, Michael F. Scott Morton, and Sumantra Ghoshal

Macroenvironmental Analysis for Strategic Management
Liam Fahey and V. K. Narayanan

Figure 2   The Strategic Management Process

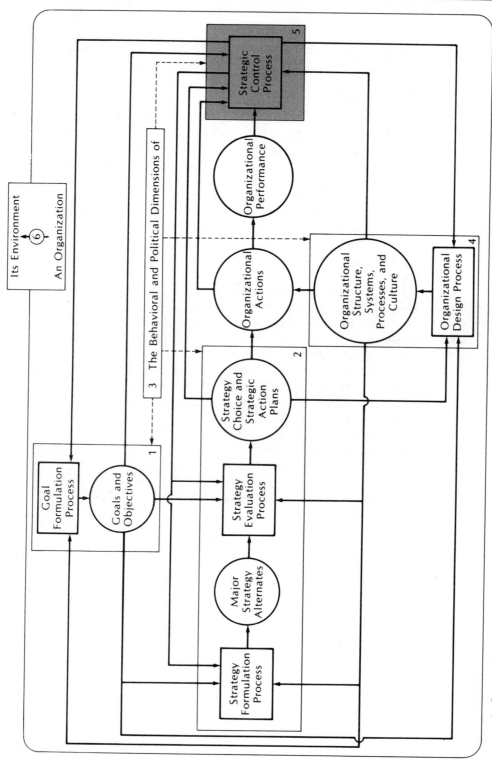

1. Setting Strategic Goals and Objectives, 2d ed.
2. Strategy Formulation: Issues and Concepts
3. Strategy Formulation: Power and Politics, 2d ed.
4. Strategy Implementation: Structure, Systems, and Process, 2d ed.
5. Strategic Control
6. Macroenvironmental Analysis for Strategic Management

The series has also been designed so that the texts within it can be used in several ways. First, the entire series can be used as a set to provide an advanced conceptual overview of the field of strategic management. Second, selected texts in the series can be combined with cases drawn from the Harvard Case Services, the Case Teaching Association, and/or the Case Research Association to create a course customized to particular instructor needs. Third, individual texts in the series can be used to supplement the conceptual materials contained in the existing text and casebooks in the field. The series thus offers the individual instructor great flexibility in designing the required business policy/strategic management course. Fourth, because of their self-contained nature, each of the texts can be used either individually or in combination with other materials as the basis for an advanced specialized course in strategic management. For instance, the text on *Strategic Control* could be used to create a state-of-the-art course on "Strategic Control Systems." Likewise, the *Macroenvironmental Analysis for Strategic Management* and *Strategy Formulation: Power and Politics* texts could be combined to create an innovative course on "Stakeholder Management." Or the text on *Setting Strategic Goals and Objectives* could be combined with a text on boards of directors to create an advanced course on the latter topic.

Finally, in concluding this Common Foreword I would like to thank my co-editor on the original series, Dan Schendel of Purdue University, for his efforts on that series. They were both substantial and valuable. Indeed, the series could not have been established as effectively as it was without him:

Charles W. Hofer
Editor
October 1985

PREFACE

This volume of the West Series in Strategic Management starts with the premise that we are facing a future that has both a greater degree of global interdependence than we have ever seen before as well as a speeded-up rate of invention and introduction of new technologies. These two broad classes of change, when coupled with the longer-term shifts in demographic, political, and economic imperatives, call into question the way organizations have chosen to exercise management control. In particular, the nature of our management control systems needs to be rethought.

Our basic argument has three elements. First, planning and control are two sides of the same coin; one without the other is not as effective as the two in combination. Thus, strategic planning needs to have strategic control.

Second, strategic control provides comparisons, and comparisons provide learning. If the organization can absorb this learning, it then embarks on a dynamic, constructive change process. In short, strategic control has at its heart the management of change.

Third, we can gain useful insight by recognizing not only a continuum of organizational types but also a continuum of changes in the external environment. These run from a more or less stable—or at least predictable—rate of change where the central task is to maintain the correct rate of momentum, all the way to a dynamic, erratic, unstable environment where a need exists for the organization to make discontinuous moves.

This position can be nicely explained in light of some recent comments made at the Strategic Management Society Conference in Barcelona (Oct. 1985) by Bruce Henderson, Michael Porter and Henry Mintzberg. All three scholars have made significant contributions to the field of strategy and our understanding of their comments is a useful way to position this book. Bruce Henderson, as the senior statesman, started the panel discussion, and among many other points, he stressed the essentially static nature of much of his earlier work, a limitation which he felt had to be redressed and therefore should be the top priority for future work. He went on to say that as economics is not much concerned with time, second order effects and feedback loops it was missing in its research base the ingredients for the insightful analysis that was needed to move the field of strategy its next step forward. He went on to challenge researchers in the field to explore the systems dynamics of competitive equilibrium, and then the related organizational factors that provide such a dynamic equilibrium.

Porter followed Henderson and agreed with the point but argued that static analysis must come first and that the much tougher dynamic conditions will have to wait for future understanding and more research. For example, we still have little to help clarify issues in determining questions of geographic scope in a global economy, let alone the dynamics of global positioning over time. Mintzberg then picked up the argument by reminding his audience that much of the writing, and indeed, practice in strategic management comes out of these static, positioning schools of thought. He went on to point out that such a conceptual base is but *one* of several powerful ways of gaining insight into effective strategic management. He fully agreed with Henderson that understanding the dynamics is critical and that furthermore, the "positioning school" seems to assume that understanding precedes action. In practice, he said there is lots of evidence that people and organizations also operate by acting first and then through such action they learn and understand. Turning the classical causality on its head produces quite different normative and prescriptive statements of how to proceed.

The common thread that runs through all three comments, in our opinion, is at the heart of this book. We must have analysis and gain all the benefits we can from that process. However, such analysis is embedded in an organization and it is necessary to explicitly recognize the additional benefits to be gained from not only rising above static analysis but also to consider the enhanced insight gained from an organizational change perspective.

In this book we treat strategic control both as a necessary addition for the strategic processes that use analytical tools, as well as part of the broader view of organizational change. These basic arguments are developed with two audiences in mind. Primarily, the book is intended as a supplemental text for advanced MBA courses in management control, strategy and policy. However, the arguments will also be of interest to managers concerned with the quality of their operational and strategic management systems.

We would like to thank several people for their help in the development of the concepts laid out in this book. We have benefited enormously from the literature cited in the pages that follow. Beyond this, we received excellent constructive suggestions from Charles Hofer and the four reviewers who commented on the first draft. They are R. Edward Freeman, University of Minnesota; Robert E. Hoskisson, Texas A&M University; Thomas H. Naylor, Duke University; and Alan J. Rowe, University of Southern California. In addition, we had valuable conversations with Professors Christopher Bartlett, Edward Bowman, Johannes Pinnings, and Howard Stevenson.

The whole project would not yet have seen the light of day but for the efforts of Terry Reagan, Heidi Brown, and Karen Humphreys. Our families, as is so often the case with authors, bore the brunt of our involvement in this book. To them goes the credit.

STRATEGIC CONTROL SYSTEMS

1

Strategic Control

In recent years, we have been experiencing a period of discontinuity in many sectors of the economy. In such situations of discontinuous change, it is especially important for an organization to have a clear view of its mission, of the external forces impinging on it, and of the progress it is making in achieving its goals. To do this well requires, among other things, systematically monitoring the organization's progress along relevant strategic dimensions and modifying the organization's strategy on the basis of this evaluation.

This process, which we call strategic control, is, in our view, an important and often missing component of the systems necessary for the effective management of an organization. A planning system that assesses the external environment and internal strengths and weaknesses will not achieve its full potential unless at the same time it also monitors and assesses the organization's progress along key strategic dimensions.

Careful monitoring of product quality and of the increasing discrimination of the consumer, particularly in light of the new standards being set by the Japanese, were two aspects of a strategic control system that would have substantially improved some sectors of American industries' response to their significant loss of market share. This book shows that while strategic control is a necessary element in the ongoing effective management of a business, it becomes vital in periods of discontinuity.

The premise of discontinuity is not new. It has been too extensively discussed by too many authors in too many recent best-sellers to leave the notion with any flavor of novelty. Drucker (1969, 1974,

1

1980), Toffler, (1970), and Naisbitt (1982), among many others, have combined insightful research with creative thinking and writing to document the irregular, nonlinear, erratic, and accelerating nature of change as we move from the industrial society to what has been variously described as the postindustrial, information, or knowledge society. These authors provide a number of examples of this turbulence or discontinuity, many manifestations of which have become obvious to us only during the past ten years. Naisbitt calls this interval "the time of the parenthesis, the time between eras." He argues that we have a long way to go before we finally emerge in a new era and that during this period, we will experience significant discontinuities in the world around us. He uses the phrase "global village" and makes the point that what happens in foreign countries and with foreign trade can effect virtually all of us, no matter what industry we happen to be in. In particular, he points out that both suppliers and customers regularly transcend national boundaries, a fact that can have sudden and sharp implications for otherwise secure domestic companies.

This book is based on the premise that turbulence and surprise are part of our lives and will stay with us. We take the viewpoint that such discontinuity is not necessarily bad but rather offers interesting opportunities to those who know how to take advantage of the change and can manage their corporations in a way that is consistent with an uncertain future. We shall attempt to redress the imbalance in the thinking of many practitioners and academicians regarding turbulence and discontinuity by emphasizing the four interrelated premises listed next. We believe that these myths of control are all too prevalent. This book attempts to challenge these myths and to develop a concept of strategic control that is appropriate for the years ahead.

We suggest that four myths of control visible in the current practice of many organizations are the following:

1. Control should be focused on the internal variables of the corporation.
   In contrast, we suggest that greater emphasis should be given to monitoring and understanding the impact of key environmental factors.
2. Surprise is bad and is to be avoided at all costs.
   We contend that this is not necessarily so; opportunism is one of the dimensions that should be stressed in good strategic control.
3. Control is a matter of fine tuning to create optimal strategic results.
   We contend that a major driving force for sound strategies is

the process of seeing what works and what does not work, by discovering what the organization really is and what it is not. Strategy is created by learning, and effective strategic control is control on the processes through which organizations learn and unlearn.

4. A control system is a set of relatively static administrative procedures.
   We argue that dynamic strategic control is necessary to manage the learning process within the organization.

Our response to these four myths of control suggests a view that is fundamentally different from that implicit in much of current practice. This is most easily seen when viewed in light of the environmental discontinuities facing the organization.

ENVIRONMENTAL DISCONTINUITIES

One useful way to begin to understand the types of discontinuities that must be taken into account in understanding the need for strategic control is to categorize them into four major areas, an approach used by many writers in the field of corporate strategy (Steiner 1979; Andrews 1980). These four areas are social, economic, technological, and political forces. Each of these environmental sectors provide powerful reasons for having an effective strategic control system—reasons that we develop in later chapters. For example, changing priorities in social and political environments, such as the increasing interest in the quality of products and the shifting role of government in the lives of ordinary citizens, require the active monitoring of qualitative variables. The changing level and shape of the social safety nets provided by governments have obvious implications for savings and investment patterns. Similarly, economic and technological discontinuities require an effective strategic control system for optimal management.

Social Forces

Today, members of the middle class not only have more disposable income as a percentage of salary but also are increasingly educated and literate. Their rate of increase in wealth seems to be greater than that of lower-income groups, and as a result, we have a bifurcation of society with a widening gap between the lower level of our society and the middle and upper classes.

The educational process needed to train individuals to allow them to move from the industrial society to the information society is difficult to achieve at the bottom of the economic and social scale. The smaller families and higher level of literacy of the middle classes make this undertaking proportionately easier, which further widens the gap. Added to this are the emergence of the two-career family and improved health standards leading to a longer expected life span. These trends have resulted in different and increasingly polarized U.S. work forces whose members have quite different expectations about their role in society and the jobs they can do than did their predecessors.

But the social change that engulfs us transcends these alterations in class structures and expectations. We are undergoing a more fundamental change that is modifying our thinking about the basic role of society and its purposes. Lodge (1975) describes this change as the emergence of a "new American ideology." Changing values about survival, justice, economy, self-fulfillment, and self-respect, combined with changes in demography, ecology, institutional systems, and technology, are progressively making obsolete traditional social norms founded on the Lockean ideology and its handmaiden, the Protestant ethic. As a result, to quote Henry Ford II, "the terms of contract between industry and society are changing. . . . How much freedom business will retain in the closing decades of this century depends on the quality of management's response to the changing expectations of the public" (in Lodge 1975). This response, in turn, depends on management's ability to continuously inspect basic assumptions, to learn from its experiences, and to adapt to the changing social and ideological mosaic. This is one of the primary tasks for strategic control.

Economic Forces

Writing in 1969, Peter Drucker showed remarkable insight in observing our transition from an international economy to a global economy (Drucker 1969). The forces of globalization, then a trickle, have since become a flood. The global capital market now moves billions of dollars every day at electronic speed. Propelled by increasing economy of scope (and scale, particularly in R&D), many industries, including almost all in the high-technology "sunrise" sectors, are becoming global in their structure. Porter (1984) calls this the transition from multidomestic to global management, where the demands of national responsiveness have to be carefully balanced against the benefits of an integrated global strategy. Even purely domestic firms are no longer exempt from the vicissitudes of global competition, as operating exposure (Lessard 1984) opens the guts of their business to the uncertainties of the floating exchange rate regime.

The question of productivity and its growth or lack thereof lies at the heart of the United States' ability to compete in the global marketplace. Organizations are discovering the need to set goals for an appropriate rate of improvement in various measures of productivity, and the related need to monitor these measures to see if improvements are indeed occurring. The much-heralded information technology explosion has the potential for enormous changes in the time and resources required to produce a given level of output in an organization. Capitalizing on this potential will distinguish the successful American companies who survive global competition from those who fall by the wayside and disappear from the organizational scene.

Technological Forces

Information technology will be one of the major forces for change over the next decade. Such technology will lead to changes in communications (voice, data, and video); computers, covering the spectrum from personal computers to large mainframes; blue-collar productivity, that is, robotics, computer-aided engineering, computer-aided manufacturing and process control; and white-collar productivity, that is, office automation (computers and communication for administrative functions) as well as management support systems in the form of decision support systems (DSS) for decision making and executive support systems for qualitative input for senior managers. All these forms of information technology can be expected to have a significant impact on the organizational design structure of firms, the way they operate, and the kinds of people and processes used within them.

All these technologies can be thought of as having three classes of effect. (These categories were first developed by Emery and Trist, 1973.) First there are the "direct" effects, such as the replacement of mechanical typesetting wtih computer-generated type. These direct effects may have most pronounced impacts on the basic structure of many industries. The benefits of scale, as we understand them now, may well diminish significantly and flexibility rather than scale may become the key source of competitive advantage. As suggested by Piore and Sabel (1984), for instance, many industries may return from assembly line to the earlier craft method of production. These and other examples of direct impacts are discussed in Chapter 8. However, it is also important to be aware of "second order, unintended" effects. We have, for example, the loss of privacy inherent in the widespread use of electronic information.

The third class of impact that Emery and Trist raise are the changes technology brings about in the ways we think about each other and the world around us. For example, we relate to each other differently, more impersonally, since we do not have to be physically near one another. At the same time, we often have greatly enlarged networks of business associates and sources of business intelligence.

In addition to information technology, other technologies are at work changing our world, perhaps the most obvious of which are genetic engineering and bioengineering. Early applications are already showing signs of impacting our culture and medicine, and provide a clear indication of the enormous changes yet to come. This list of technologies is continually expanding, and no signs are evident that the rate of invention and application is slowing down, let alone stopping.

Political Forces

Worldwide shifts in policy that have major impacts on other nations are already a reality. Instant satellite communication plus global interconnections in trade and finance have tied the nations of the world closely together. Political events in one corner of the globe can have almost immediate ramifications elsewhere. The sovereignty-at-bay hypothesis has clearly fallen by the wayside. The OPEC price hike is still sufficiently recent to make elaboration of this point unnecessary. The political dimensions of international trade lead to great uncertainty in an organization's external environment with enormously high positives and negatives. Organizations also have to deal with their home government's activity within national boundaries. In the United States, the government's de facto industrial policy moves the country from regulation to deregulation and from protection to free market in an irregular pattern. These swings are relatively sudden and frequently extreme.

EFFECTS OF ENVIRONMENTAL DISCONTINUITIES

These four sets of forces have provided the pressures for the discontinuities that we have experienced thus far and which will certainly continue for the next several years. Understanding and staying in touch with changes in these underlying forces is exceedingly important. By being constantly aware of changes in these critical parameters and by anticipating how one's strategic position might thereby change, one has the basis for making use of the changes. Rapid change and discontinuity have become a way of life in the 1980s, and since we see every indication that this will continue in the decades ahead (Piore and Sabel 1984), such change represents an enormous opportunity. This book presents a way to deal with these phenomena so that those who understand them gain an added advantage over those who do not.

Virtually every issue of the business press provides an example of the impact of one or more of these forces on a company or industry. For example, new technology and gradual deregulation are having an enormous impact on the financial services industry. At one point, the image of banking was one of financial experts operating behind regulatory barriers with armies of clerks and sophisticated "relationship" lending officers. Banks are now part of the financial services industry, in which they compete with insurance companies, brokers, and even retailers such as Sears, Roebuck and Company. Electronic funds transfer systems, automatic tellers, and people willing to treat money as a commodity have all combined to make the comfortable history of banking take on a whole new look. To caricature the situation, one could describe the historical position as one wherein elegant bankers in the front office made loans on the strength of thier relationship and knowledge of particular companies, while the back office was a sort of factory where managers from the Ford Motor Company were brought in to deal with the "factory" problems in the back office. When technology moved from the back office to the customer in the form of automatic tellers, the transformation of banking was well and truly under way.

The next generation of change has taken place much more recently, as can be evidenced from the following story. The advent of personal computers and the extraordinary developments in communications cost led a young MBA student in one of the major banks to develop a piece of software for personal computers that became part of a product sold by the bank to help corporate treasurers manage their corporation's money. Personal computers could be linked into the bank's electronic funds transfer system, which closely tied customers to the bank, to the bank's benefit. This service enabled customers to move their money quickly, cheaply, and to the optimal location to benefit the corporation. The sale of this product provided a new source of revenue to the bank. Suddenly, the bank found itself generating a significant amount of income from a service provided by the bank rather than from the money from which it had traditionally gained its revenue.

A planning system based on the status quo, which measures the traditional variables that have served banks so well over the years, would clearly be inadequate in view of the discontinuities involved in competition from organizations other than banks and profits from sources other than lending relationships. In such environments, incremental planning systems provide a completely wrong view of competition and of products. A traditional incremental control system that monitors financial results in a mature industry can easily fail to note the new key variables associated with the kind of discontinuity involved in a case like this. A strategic control system is designed to identify and monitor just such discontinuities and address such changes.

Many discontinuities are more directly government instigated. The AT&T breakup is clearly one such major discontinuity in the communications field, but others have occurred in such industries as airlines and trucking, and a host related to changes in health and safety regulations.

Not all discontinuities are caused by the government. Political, social, and technical forces combined to provide an opportunity for Japan in the automobile business that they were not slow to capitalize on. Customers' desire for quality, the cost of gasoline, the cost of cars, as well as the social acceptability of smaller cars and smaller families all combined to help Japan significantly. However, their superior ability to assemble and digest the facts of the situation and put together a composite balanced picture allowed them to focus on high-quality, low-cost products. American firms did not absorb the implications of the changes in the wind—for example, that compromises on quality had become unacceptable to many consumers. To make it clear to employees that quality matters, a control system must be developed that puts the quality measure clearly in front of management and the workers. Such a control system goes well beyond the mangement accounting dimensions of the past and should be part of the strategic control system of such an organization.

In all these cases, hindsight allows us to see not only that more creative planning systems are required but also that in periods of turbulence, thinking about and learning from new measures for monitoring performance are necessary. We are arguing that one should not fight change but should learn from it. Good strategic control should emphasize how to thrive on change and discontinuity. These factors should be seen as opportunities, not as undesirable threats.

One of the points of strategic control is that it is located in the middle ground of the following continuum:[1]

---

1. We are indebted to Charles Hofer for suggesting this particular set of words.

Control Type 1 UNCONTROLLABLE	Control Type 2 INFLUENCEABLE	Contol Type 3 CONTROLLABLE
No action of the firm will affect events in this arena, e.g., broad societal changes.	Corporation can influence stake-holders' behavior, e.g., industry dynamics.	Corporation has dominant cause-and-effect power, e.g., internal incentive scheme.

The four sets of forces discussed in the preceding pages are, from a company viewpoint, virtually uncontrollable. However, they are a crucial element of strategic control. Such Type 1 control requires the organization to actively monitor these broad external forces and stay alert to responding to them at the appropriate point. For example, with the increasing number of dual-career families, new work practices may have to be put in place to capture the relevant expertise for the benefit of the organization's stakeholders. These forces are uncontrollable, but they have an imperative that demands that the organization respond.

This response is Type 2 control, which we are calling strategic control, a concept subsequently defined. Such control has an underpinning of Type 3 control, which is the classical budgetary and operational control that most modern organizations have developed to a considerable level of sophistication.

Not all firms are in equally turbulent situations. Although change is almost all-pervasive, in some industries, such as cement and bulk chemicals, change has been more linear and less erratic. In others, such a semiconductors, aerospace, and specialty petrochemicals, change has been especially turbulent and discontinuous. At the level of implementation, strategic control would indeed be different depending on the rate and nature of change faced by the firm. However, at the conceptual level, the basic premise of strategic control remains unaffected. The four sets of forces described earlier have set the world in motion, and partly because of uncontrollable events, a need exists for strategic control. No company, however safe and secure in quiet backwaters it may appear, can escape the pervasive nature of changes brought about by these forces. It is no longer sufficient for any firm to simply measure itself over time, comparing present performance with the past. Comparisons now always have to be made against the competition and relative to the rest of the world.

DEFINITIONS OF STRATEGIC CONTROL

Having elaborated on the situation that causes us to be concerned with the subject of strategic control, we move now to a definition of what we mean by that term. At the conceptual level, the issue is clear. The word *strategy* comes from *strategos*, a Greek word meaning "art of the general." The dictionary definition of *control* is "to exercise control over or to test or verify using a standard of comparison." Strategic control from this viewpoint therefore becomes testing or verifying the art of the general manager. However, at the practical level, the meaning of strategic control is more obscure. The obscurity comes when one tries to take an apparently straight forward definition and translate it into actual implementable terms in a real organization. We discuss this implementation question in the chapters that follow.

The system necessary to exercise control is defined as that combination of components which act together to maintain actual performance close to a desired set of performance specifications. In the management context, we define a strategic control system as a system to support managers in assessing the relevance of the organization's strategy to its progress in the accomplishment of its goals, and when discrepancies exist, to support areas needing attention.

An interesting point is that the planning departments of many organizations are separate from the comptroller's department. The assumption seems to have been made that the comptroller's department exercises control, and the planning department plans. Apparently, not many people perceive that the two being disconnected is a major failing in the management systems in such firms. That they are two sides of the same coin can be highlighted by the following argument. If we do not control against our plans, we will never know if they have been achieved. Similarly, if we control only against a fixed, rigid set of objectives, we can miss the need to make the changes that mean survival. Rearranging the deck chairs on the Titanic into straight rows on the evening before the collision is the often-used analogy for such limited control behavior.

Strategic control, however, has different characteristics depending on the state of the external environment. We find it useful to break the state of the world into the two broad categories that are described below.

Controlling the Strategic Momentum

Controlling strategic momentum focuses on the maintenance of a particular strategic direction while coping with environmental turbulence and change. The essence of this control is to reconfirm organizationally that the critical environmental assumptions behind the particular strategy are still valid (i.e., that the strategy can evolve within the established rules that have previously governed it). Here, the underlying strategic assumptions are still valid, and the business is still being managed through adherence to these assumptions despite much turbulence and disturbance. The basic continuity of the business is still credible, and one can hence speak of an extrapolation of the given strategy, even though a lot of operational changes may be taking place. The challenge here is to manage the buffeting of the given strategy and to maintain the strategy on course.

Such momentum control is appropriate when the forces both outside and inside the organization are relatively peaceful. Strong eddies and crosscurrents may well exist, but by maintaining vigorous momentum, the organization can move successfully toward its goals.

Controlling the Strategic Leap

Under some conditions of discontinuity maintaining momentum will simply not get the organization to the position it has to be in to successfully survive. Here, the challenge is to reset the trajectory of the strategy as well as to decide on the relative levels of thrust and momentum for the new strategic direction. The critical underlying assumptions that underpin the strategy are no longer viable, and the rules that govern the strategy must be redefined. This situation involves a mental leap to define the new rules and to cope with any emerging new environmental factors. Such a recalibrating of strategy requires a personal liberation from traditional thinking, an ability to change one's mind-set, and confronting the challenge of creating advantage out of discontinuity. The question now is how to achieve a quantum leap in one's strategy to capitalize on emerging environmental turbulence. One must proceed by redefining the rules rather than by clinging to the unrealistic hope that the old rules are still valid.

In many ways, these conditions can be thought of as requiring almost a wartime mentality. It is a time when only the organization that has both the internal motivation, strengths, and skills as well as a sound strategic position will be the one to reward its stakeholders. A global competitive environment is not one to reward those who cannot change to match the times.

Robert Anthony's important early work provides some further perspective. In a classic book, *Planning and Control Systems: A Framework for Analysis* (1965), Anthony defines *strategic planning* as a process having to do with the formulation of long-range plans of a policy nature that change the character or direction of the organization. He also maintains that in an idustrial company, this includes "all planning that affects the goals of the company; policies of all types; the acquisition and disposition of major facilities, divisions, or subsidiaries; the markets to be served, and distribution channels for serving them. Strategic planning decisions affect the physical, financial and organization framework within which operations are carried out" (Anthony 1965, 10). *Management control,* on the other hand, is defined by Anthony as the process by which management ensures that the organization carries out its strategies effectively and efficiently. He goes on to define *operational control* as the process of ensuring that specific tasks are carried out effectively and efficiently. Anthony points out that these three processes cannot be separated by sharp boundaries, because each one shades into the other. However, he argues that strategic planning sets the guidelines for management control, and management control sets the guidelines for operational control.

Given the way that management terminology has changed in the years since Anthony wrote his book, one can make the hierarchical point somewhat clearer by labeling the three areas strategic planning, tactical planning, and operational planning. However, in view of our assertion that planning and control are two sides of the same coin, we describe the spectrum of management decisions as shown in Figure 1.1.

The schematic suggested in the figure implies two kinds of links in an organization's planning and control systems. First, each system must be independently integrated across the strategic, tactical and operational levels. How this might be done has already been suggested by many authors. For example, Hofer and Schendel (1978) and Hax and Majluf (1985) have provided excellent and detailed descriptions of how to integrate the planning process across the

Figure 1.1   Linkages Within and Between Organizational Planning and Control Systems across the Spectrum of Management Decisions

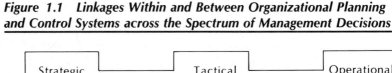
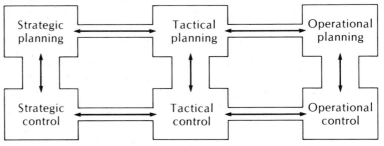

different levels. Similarly Lorange and Vancil (1977) have pointed out how operational and strategic control systems can be tied together through the use of "strategic programs".

The second set of links suggested in the schematic are between the planning and control systems within each of the three decision categories. These are the links on which we focus in this book. As Anthony points out, these categories of management decisions differ along many dimensions, including the issues they deal with, the time frame they are concerned with, and the level of detail that is involved (Gorry and Scott Morton 1971). However, we argue that in all instances, both a planning dimension and a control dimension must be present if the organization is to move through time successfully. After all, the analysis of why one did not reach one's goals is what provides the necessary insight that permits successful replanning and repositioning for the appropriate next steps. In many ways, this learning process becomes built into the corporation and leads to a much more productive view of settling on and achieving strategic direction. The firm can thereby become appropriately opportunistic as new environmental changes are sensed, and it can then engage in proactive adaptation, not merely defensive reaction after the fact.

Equally important, the process of comparing actual with plan can generate the energy required in any human organization to overcome resistance to change and to acknowledge mistakes. The energies thus released are a significant resource in an effective organization.

Thus, strategic planning and strategic control deal primarily with setting basic strategic direction within the environmental contexts in which the firm finds itself. Often, this implies heavy emphasis on understanding how critical environmental factor might impact an initial strategic direction. In such a case, strategic control deals with the follow-up of critical environmental assumptions and changes in these, thus sensitizing the organization to anticipate discontinuities.

Tactical planning and control, on the other hand, can be thought of as dealing more with how one implements the intended strategic direction within the context of the strategic plan. The issue here might be the development of a strategic program for particular product-market niches, which would involve activating internal capabilities and resources to pursue the chosen direction. Tactical control in this context might focus on assessing how the environment reacts to one's tactical plans as they unfold by monitoring competitor or customer reactions, in addition to seeing how well one is doing on such output measures as milestones, market share gains, and so forth.

Operating planning and control can be thought of as near-term blueprints for the activities in the firm—dealing with what is going on today to achieve both the near-term and long-term success of the firm. Control in this case may be concerned with the detailed achievement of specific deliverables. Such deliverables will often run the full gamut from quantitative to qualitative and will normally be associated with specific individuals.

We would like to make one more distinction in terminology at this stage. Strategy is a concept, theoretically, for the chief executive officer (the "general"). However, the term has become debased. Every function is now elevated in importance by associating it with the word *strategy*. Thus, for example, terms such as strategic manufacturing, strategic marketing, and financial strategy have become common in both theory and practice. In these cases, perhaps the word *positioning* is more appropriate. Major long-term positioning moves should doubtlessly be created and implemented in the context of every function and by every manager in the operation, no matter how lowly. Thus, the theoretical misuse of the term *strategy* has emphasized an important point, namely that all levels and positions in an organization have a real opportunity for creative moves. For example, for a firm to be effective, a need exists for the heads of responsibility centers such as marketing and manufacturing to position their pieces of the organization effectively for the longer term, albeit within the larger context of the organization. In that sense, the truly excellent division manager or functional manager has a chance to display the "art of the general." Even in their own constrained worlds, such managers have an opportunity to find the correct place or manner in which to succeed. Division managers also need to monitor local strategic progress, to learn as they move toward their chosen goals, and to reassess whether their goals still remain valid. This is particularly true in light of the opportunities presented at all levels by the shifting forces of the contemporary environment. Such monitoring and learning is the main function of strategic control, and done well, it can make a significant difference to an organization. A persuasive argument has been made by many (e.g., Pascale and Athos 1981) that this is one reason why the Japanese have successfully taken over so many markets from the West.

METHODS OF STRATEGY FORMULATION

We have argued that strategic planning and strategic control are two sides of the same coin and that one cannot be effective without the other. This argument implies that the strategic control system must fit the firm's overall approach to strategy formulation, for otherwise the two systems cannot be meshed into an integrated management process. In looking at organizations, one observes a wide variety of methods by which the explicit or implicit strategy of a firm is crated (Chakravarthy and Lorange 1984). Even within the Fortune 1,000, some firms have formal, "scientific," elaborate planning systems, while other, whose CEOs act as though strategic intuition combined with a one-year budget is an entirely adequate combination for their needs, operate with minimal formal strategic planning. We are not aware of any comprehensive study that sheds light on the type of strategic management that is more appropriate for a given type of organization. An interesting point is that even among the "excellent companies" of Peters and Waterman (1982), almost no consistency exists in the ways in which they approach strategic questions or even strategic thinking.

Given the enormously varied way in which organizations approach strategy, the expectation is that their approaches to strategic control will be equally diverse. And given that the differences in methods of strategic planning reflect differences in strategic control that are fundamental in nature, at least at the level of implementation, an appropriate avenue is to address this issue in this introductory chapter and to lay out a framework to understand how strategic control would vary to fit a firm's strategic planning process. In this effort, we start from the premise that for an organization to benefit from strategic control, it must have thought about its strategy. Further, the clearer the firm's understanding is about its strategy, the easier it will be to identify the key variables, and the better the strategic control system.

Various typologies have been proposed for classifying an organization's approach to strategy. These range from the simple "prospector, analyzer, defender, reactor" classification of Miles and Snow (1978) to considerably more elaborate schemes. (See Chaffee [1985] for a comprehensive review of various approaches to strategy.) Recently, the suggestion has also been made that strategy, by definition, is multidimensional and situational, and therefore cannot be typed or classified (Hambrick 1983) but rather must be understood with reference to its context (Pettigrew 1983). However, what is important for us is not the way strategy is actually formed but the way the organization intends to formulate strategy. Identifying the difference between intended and realized strategy (Mintzberg 1983) is one of the key functions of strategic control. The intended strategy, or more accurately, the process of arriving at the intended strategy, we suggest, can be categorized without undue oversimplification of reality.

An organization's strategy formulation process reflects its assumptions about both its external and internal environments. In the external environment, it either assumes linearity and continuity or acknowledges the possibility of discontinuous breaks. If strategy is the means for identifying where one wants to go as well as how to get there, with an assumption of continuity, the identification of the desired state (where to go) becomes relatively easy, since it can be defined by simple extrapolation. Without an assumption of continuity, delineation of one's goals becomes considerably more difficult, because where one wants to be depends on what the world will look like, and with the possibility of discontinuities, assessment of the external environment becomes much more complex. In our view, both continuities and discontinuities are at work. Our approach establishes a way to look at continuities within the context of a broader picture within which discontinuities can be assessed.

Similarly, for the internal environment, the organization either assumes a monolithic homogeneity so that the "where to go" question (strategy formulation) can be separated from the "how to get there" issue (strategy implementation), or assumes that the two are interrelated because of internal heterogeneity arising from cognitive limits and political agendas of the members. The first assumption reflects the "rational" view elaborated in Allison (1971); the second includes bureaucratic and political models.

These wide-ranging assumptions about internal and external environments, coupled with differences in corporate culture between organizations, have fundamental implications for the type of approach to strategic control that will be successful. As mentioned, a major distinction should be made between strategic control approaches that are intended for situations in which the nature of the environmental changes are predominantly of the type that can be characterized as linear (i.e., where the change process is one of continuity) versus those strategic control approaches that can be applied when environmental changes are predominantly of the discontinuity type. In the former case (i.e., with linear changes and continuity), the strategic control process we call momentum control, or "peacetime" control, can be employed. This approach consists of emphasis on maintaining a stable evolutionary path within an organization by ameliorating problems and addressing deviations from normal development on a steady, ongoing basis. Momentum builds up in an organization as a result of the ongoing dynamics of making and delivering its goods and services to the marketplace. Such a "flywheel" can be guided into new paths through the efforts of its managers. This redirection can be made immeasurably easier if it is shared widely within the firm. The process of strategic planning in "peacetime" is about maintaining momentum and modifying direction. Strategic control is an integral part of this, as we show in the following chapters.

Even though environmental changes may at times be large under peacetime conditions, seeing how a future direction will evolve from the past is relatively easy. Consequently, momentum control is concerned with facilitating a smooth evolution, grounded in past strategic positions.

"Leap" control, or wartime startegic control, on the other hand, is based on the assumption that the environment is changing with such a degree of discontinuity that the normal rules of the game no longer hold, and the evolutionary mode of momentum control is no longer adequate. Strategic planning and control in wartime has to do wtih making leaps, causing the organization to make a discontinuous move. The direction and extent of the organization's leap into new markets or new technologies are sometimes based on existing strengths that were previously scattered across the organization. GE's declared leap into the factory of the future is an example. In other cases, such a leap can mean acquiring new skills, such as the Harris Corporation's leap from mechanical typesetting into the electronic world of information technology.

Under these circumstances, a more open-ended, free-for-all strategic control process must be put in place, with heavy emphasis on a redefinition of how things should be done and on developing novel and unorthodox approaches—in short, the firm must operate in a wartime mode. Based on our reading of the academic and practitioner literature on strategy and on our own consulting and research experience, we detect eight approaches to strategic control that are in use. In practice, any given organization will use a blend of some or all of these approaches. Table 1.1 suggests a typology that groups these approaches according to their underlying assumptions about the organization and its environment.

In delineating this framework, we do not intend to suggest that

**Table 1.1 Types of Strategic Control
Based on Assumptions about the Nature of Environmental Changes**

Strategic Momentum Control •Peacetime Control •Linear Changes and Continuity	Strategic Leap Control •Wartime Control •Discontinuity
1. Classical Responsibility Center Control	1. Strategic Issue Management
2. Controlling Underlying Assumptions	2. Stategic Field Analysis
3. Controlling Generic Strategy	3. Computer-Based Modeling
	4. Scenario Planning

one method of strategic control is superior to another. Indeed, the classical methods are probably much more in use today. Our objective is merely to construct a typology for discussing how strategic control might vary depending on which appproach to strategy is used in the organization.

To proceed further, evolving a nomenclature for the different categories will be useful. Like all other authors in search of a nomenclature, we have the problem of finding labels that are short, symbolic, and meaningful. We recognize that the terminology of *"momentum"* or *peacetime* and *"leap"* or *wartime* can be faulted on various grounds (including inappropriate dramatization), but it serves the purpose of highlighting the basic difference that we think is the key to strategic control—the difference of approach based on assumptions of the nature of environmental change. We suggest that the concept of strategic control is universal but that its actual implementation will be widely different in peacetime and in times of severe change.

The content of Table 1.1 is discussed more fully in Chapters 4 and 5, respectively. For our purposes, at this stage we merely wish to make the points that effective strategic control will vary depending on the approach to strategy that is used by the organization, and that such approaches can be readily, if somewhat too dichotomously, grouped according to underlying assumptions about the nature of the environment and about the organization.

OUTLINE OF THE BOOK

In this book, we articulate our view of what modern strategic control means, based on the definitions of the term developed in this chapter. The presentation is organized broadly in two parts. In the first part, consisting of the first three chapters, we develop and elaborate the conceptual apparatus that undergirds our views on strategic control. The second part, consisting of the remaining six chapters, deals with the operational issues of how strategic control can be implemented under different environmental and organizational contexts. The conceptual discussions in the first part, we believe, may be helpful for readers to interpret our operational suggestions in the light of their own particular circumstances. This is crucial, since fundamental to our thesis is the notion that the nature of strategic control is contingent on the context and that no "one best way" exists. What we therefore wish to achieve is to highlight the broad logic of strategic control rather that to merely provide the reader with a specific set of do's and don'ts.

In this introductory chapter, we have suggested that a central objective of strategic control is to develop the organization's learning and adaptive abilities. In Chapter 2, we review some of the existing perspectives on organizational change and describe a simple model of adaptation as an interacting process of sensitizing, learning, and institutionalization. To achieve the objectives of strategic control, one needs to understand the mechanisms that influence these processes, since through those mechanisms the firm's ability to adapt can be enhanced.

In Chapter 3, the external environment is introduced into the model. We argue that the adaption and learning processes are driven by organizational perception of the environment and that such perceptions are in turn affected by factors such as the structure of the organization, internal slack, and information systems. These factors act as filters that influence the way organizations enact or interpret the environment. As mentioned earlier in this chapter, we view controlling the learning process of the organization as a key task of the strategic control system. The model of organizational learning developed in Chapters 2 and 3 suggests a set of mechanisms through which the firm can control its learning processes. In the final part of Chapter 3 we specifically identify these mechanisms which, according to the view presented in this book, constitute the principal leverage points for operationalizing strategic control.

The next two chapters deal primarily with operational issues. In Chapter 4, we develop the basics of a strategic control system in the context of a relatively stable environment. The key strategic task in such a context is to maintain strategic momentum. In this chapter, we discuss the three broad approaches to momentum control indicated in table 1.1, viz, classical responsibility center control, control based on assessing critical underlying key success factors, and control on the basic generic strategies. For each of these approaches, we identify the key variables that form the focus of strategic control and suggest how those variables can be measured and influenced. We conclude the chapter by suggesting how all these approaches can be integrated with a contingency-based system of strategic momentum control.

In Chapter 5, we turn our attention to the situation of a turbulent and discontinuous environment: a condition that may call for strategic leaps by the organization. We suggest that some of the emerging approaches to strategy, such as strategic issue management, strategic field analysis, systems modeling, and scenario-based planning methods, are particularly appropriate under these circumstances. We briefly describe these methods and suggest that they provide early warning systems for sensitizing management to impending changes.

Chapter 6 discusses the concept of strategic control in the specific context of a diversified firm. Strategic control, we suggest, is especially important for effective management of diversification for two reasons. First, diversification adds value only as long as the firm enjoys some benefits of synergy (i.e., some economies of scope). Strategic control is essential to continuously monitor the potential synergies that may be available and to review the extent that the benefits of such synergies are actually obtained by the firm. Second, a diversified firm needs to maintain a balance between differentiating the strategies of its various components so that they are consistent with the demands of their unique task environments, and integrating the strategies of the different components so as to provide internal strategic and administrative consistency within the total organization. There are costs and benefits of both internal and external consistencies, and strategic control is necessary to maintain an optimal balance between the two.

Chapter 7 deals with operationalizing strategic control (i.e., how to carry out the necessary corrective strategic changes stemming from the sensitization that has taken place regarding changes in critical environmental assumptions). Also, this chapter deals with the institutionalization of such changes. We discuss this in terms of a model for impacting and strengthening the change process based on taking advantage of the pressures built up in the organization as a result of the sensitizing process. Follow-up approaches for institutionalization are then discussed, such as embedding, changing culture, and so on. Finally, we discuss this as a hierarchical phenomenon, stressing that the institutionalization of change at one organizational level should be seen not merely as the culmination of strategic control at this level but also as a basis for sensitizing lower organizational levels to the need for change. We suggest that the degree to which this vertical set of links builds up needs for strategic change in the hierarchy differs depending on the nature of the organization and its diversity.

Chapter 8 discusses the roles of decision support systems and information technology in strategic control. Here, we deal with incorporating the latest computer-based technological tools and discuss the user dimension of this, pinpointing necessary modifications in the strategic control processes to avert the possibility that incorporation of these tools might lead to dysfunctional consequences. Finally, in Chapter 9, the concluding chapter, we discuss several implications for future development of strategic control, based on our perception of major trends regarding strategic, behavioral, and technological factors driving strategic control. In this chapter, we also illustrate the CEO's role in developing good strategic management.

2

Strategic Control and Organizational Change

INTRODUCTION

Strategic control, as discussed in Chapter 1, is a necessary complement to strategic planning. The monitoring and feedback mechanism of the overall strategic management process engenders change through an understanding of where and how things are not as they should be. From this perspective, strategic control is managing change—change at the strategic level that affects the objectives, direction, character, or domain of the company.

Further, we have also argued that the nature of strategic control differs significantly depending on the nature of change that the organization has to cope with. When change is relatively stable and evolutionary, strategic control involves controlling the organizational momentum acquired on the strength of past strategic positions. On the other hand, when change is turbulent and discontinuous, a fundamental redefinition of the firm's strategic position may be called for, and strategic control, under such a situation, may involve controlling the leap form one strategic state to another. Such a polarized dichotomization may be overly simplistic, but it is useful to highlight the different nature of strategic control under different environmental assumptions. It is also suggestive of how the processes of strategic control may vary, depending on which of the two states more closely resembles the operating environment of the firm. In actual practice, certain components of the firm may need momentum control while others may be in a state of leap, and the overall objective of the strategic control system must include managing change under both these states.

In this and the following chapters, our objective is to identify the

21

key organizational variables through which managers can influence the strategic control process in their firms. The central thrust of our argument is that strategic control is exercised by first making the firm more sensitive to external changes. Such sensitization facilitates organizational learning and adaptive change. To identify the leverage points for exercising strategic control, one must therefore look to the mechanisms that affect the sensitizing and learning processes in firms.

We view the process of organizational change as both induced and autonomous: Change can be achieved by proactive actions, and it can also emerge as an outcome of current environmental and organizational contexts (Burgelman 1983). The autonomous component of strategic change is influenced by one set of mechanisms, while the emergent component is affected by another set of variables. To achieve strategic control, managers must attend to both the sets—with differing priorities depending on whether the objective is to manage strategic momentum or to control strategic leaps.

We build our arguments in two stages. In this chapter, we review some of the current perspectives on organizational change and propose a simple model of organizational adaptation as an interacting process of sensitizing, change, and institutionalization. At this stage, we ignore the role of the external environment and focus instead only on processes that are internal to the firm. Scanning and experimenting are identified as the principal instruments for sensitizing organizations, ensuring appropriate level of commitment on the part of a critical mass of organizational members is seen as the primary vehicles for creating change, and socialization and value consensus are proposed as key mechanisms for institutionalizing change. These, we suggest, are the main leverage points through which managers can enhance the adaptive capabilities of their firms.

In Chapter 3, we introduce the external environment into the model and suggest that factors such as organizational structure, internal slack, and information systems affect how the environment will be *perceived* by the organizational members. These perceptions about the environment, rather than any objective reality, drive the sensitizing, learning, and institutionalization processes. Further, we argue that these perceptions can be managed, at least partially, by controlling a set of organizational filters that affect the way organizations enact or interpret the environment. These filters therefore provide another set of leverage points for exercising strategic control.

In both this chapter and the next, our arguments are theoretical and abstract. The principal objective of this book is to develop applied theory (i.e., a description of steps in a process to arrive at a certain end). We address this task in Chapters 5 through 8. However, we believe that anchoring applied theory in an explicit conceptual framework can provide more depth of understanding and can facilitate a more critical and discriminating evaluation of the prescriptive suggestions. This chapter and the next develop the theoretical apparatus on which our concept of strategic control is rooted. Such an abstract discussion of theory, we recognize, may enhance the entry barrier to the applied chapters that follow, but our hope is that the reader who stoically plows through will, at the end, find the journey to have been fruitful.

PERSPECTIVES ON ORGANIZATIONAL CHANGE

Strategic control, as a topic of inquiry, is a relatively new one. The phenomenon of organizational change, in contrast, has attracted the attention of many researchers and scholars for well over three decades. Given our view that the two topics are closely interrelated, brief discussion on the topic of organizational change is an useful starting point for developing an understanding of the concept of strategic control.

The literature on organizational change is both rich and conflicting. Attention of authors belonging to a diverse range of academic disciplines has led to the development of many perspectives and theories of why and how organizations change (or do not change). An exhaustive review of this literature is beyond the scope of this book (interested readers can find such a review and also a comprehensive bibliography in Goodman and Associates 1982). For our purposes, it is sufficient to highlight some of the key concepts and to relate them to our views on strategic control.

Interest in organizational change was one of the many consequences of the open systems view of organizations that emerged in the 1930s and which soon became the dominant paradigm in the field of organization and management theory. This view holds that the effectiveness of an organization depends on how appropriately the characteristics of the organization are matched with the attributes of its environment. To the extent that the environmental characteristics change, and often turbulently so, as we have discussed in Chapter 1, the continued effectiveness of the organization depends on its ability to monitor such changes and to maintain the fit through appropriate modifications either in the environment or in its own attributes. Prior to the emergence of the open systems view, the issue of organizational adaptation was not considered relevant, since the dominant belief was that "one best way" existed for managing organizations, and primary attention of management scholars was devoted to finding universalistic "principles of management" that embodied that "one best way." Thus, to Weber, bureaucratic structures and controls were appropriate for all organizational settings (Henderson and Parsons 1947), just as to Taylor (1911), the principles of scientific management were universal in their applicability. Once having found the "one best way," firms needed no further changes. In contrast, the open systems view posited adaptation and change as key factors for ongoing effectiveness of organizations.

Adaptation: Rational Versus Natural Selection

Various theories have been proposed to explain how organizational adaptation takes place, the principal difference between them lying in the extent to which managers are perceived to be able to influence the adaptation process.

Scholars in the field of business policy have argued that managers can and do influence organizational change through creating and changing organizational purpose (Barnard 1938; Selznick 1957; Andrews 1980), through analytical planning systems (Ansoff 1965; Ackoff 1970), and through modifications in their structures and processes in response to changes in the external environment (Chandler 1962; Lawrence and Lorsch 1967; Thompson 1967). Among organization theorists, this view has been advocated by Child (1972), who has argued that the dominant coalitions (roughly, the senior managers) in organizations have considerable autonomy to choose among strategic alternatives, thereby enabling organizations to adapt proactively, rather than merely to accommodate to uncontrollable changes. They can choose the environment (i.e., industry or market) to operate in, the technology to adopt, and the structure and control systems that are appropriate to deal with the size and diversity of their operations. Besides, they can also manipulate or control their environments. Collectively, these abilities to exercise strategic choice allow organizations to creatively adapt to environmental contingencies.

A different perspective on the adaptation process is offered by the natural selection model of organizations. In essence, proponents of this view (e.g., Hannan and Freeman 1977; Aldrich 1979) argue that both internal structural arrangements and external constraints create inertial pressures on organizations that substantially limit the ability of managers to exercise any strategic choice. Besides, managers' perceptions of reality are often highly homogeneous, which makes truly proactive strategic change improbable. These authors view adaptation as an evolutionary process that proceeds along the three stages of variation, selection, and retention. First, variations occur among a population of organizations through random changes, emulation, or innovation. From the perspective of populations of organizations, the source of variation is irrelevant, for all it does is provide a pool of variations from which, in the second step, the environment differentially selects one or some, and organizations excluded from selection fail, thereby excluding their variation from the pool. In the third step, the selected variations are retained. From this evolutionary perspective, therefore, and individual organization's ability to adapt is of little importance, since it has limited effect on determining the population of surviving organizations.

Similar divergence in views also exists with regard to the process of organizational change. On the one hand, authors such as Ansoff (1965) and Steiner (1979) have proposed models that view the process as highly analytical and rational. Change, in these models, arises from analysis of gaps between organizational aspirations and capabilities, and from actions to meet those gaps through the processes of planning and control. On the other hand, authors such as Weick (1969) and Cohen, March, and Olsen (1972) have viewed organizations as loosely coupled systems, or as garbage cans, where the process of choice involves many activities besides making choices. "For example, [in the process of making choices] standard operating procedures are executed; truth is defined, history is interpreted, glory and blame are distributed, self-interests are discovered, and people enjoy themselves. These complexities and the ambiguities of intention, understanding, history, and organization together place severe limitations on the complete rational cycle of choice; each connection in the cycle of choice is at times severed by the extreme ambiguity present in organizational settings" (Goodman and Associates 1982, 33). In these views of organizations, streams of problems, solutions, participants, and choice opportunities float around, and although a chance confluence of these streams can and does produce organizational change, the processes by which such changes arise are entirely different from the analytical and rational process assumed in the strategy literature.

Evolutionary and Revolutionary Models of Change

If theoretical and normative views about organizational adaptation differ so widely, empirical observations and inductive inferences about organizational change are no less divergent. At one extreme, researchers such as Quinn (1980) have found the process to be incremental, with change emerging "step by step from an iterative process in which the organization probes the future, experiments, and learns from a series of partial (incremental) commitments rather than through global formulations of total strategies" (58). This, as we shall discuss in greater detail in Chapter 5, is closely akin to change under the peacetime assumption of managing momentum. Miller and Friesen (1984), on the other hand, have proposed the quantum view of organizational change, where long periods of the maintenance of a given configuration are punctuated by brief periods of multifaceted and concerted transition to a new one. In other words, change is seen as arising from strategic leaps.

The field of organizational design (OD) reflects a similar lack of consensus with regard to the process of organizational change. In this field, too, views about modes of change span a wide spectrum from discrete upheavals (Hornstein, Bunker, Burke, Gindes, and Lewicki 1971) to gradual evolution (Bennis, Benne, and Chin 1969). Inherent in most of the planned change models, however, is the framework of unfreeze-change-refreeze first proposed by Lewin (1952) and subsequently explored by Lippitt, Watson, and Westley (1958), Beckhard and Harris (1977), and Schein (1969). This model views change as a discrete phenomenon to be achieved through the intervention of an external change agent. Organizational change, in this view, is akin to breakdown maintenance: to be undertaken as and when the input, transformation, and output processes of an organization cease to be congruent (Nadler 1981).

Self-design, or the notion of designing into the organization a flexibility that facilitates continuous redesign, is a relatively new thrust in the field of OD. Hedberg, Nystrom, and Starbuck (1976), in a pioneering work, have suggested that organizational design should be more like erecting tents than palaces. The metaphor emphasizes the need for flexibility, creativity, immediacy, and initiative rather than authority, clarity, decisiveness, or responsiveness in designing adaptive organizations. This notion of self-design is consistent with the emerging concept of organizations as interpretation and learning systems (Draft and Weick 1984), a concept that lies at the core of our views on strategic control.

An Emerging Synthesis

As indicated at the outset, this brief review of the vast and rich literature on organizational change is neither comprehensive nor evaluative. Our objective was not to inform the reader of the state of the art on the topic but merely to highlight some of the different perspectives that exist in the normative, theoretical, and empirical literature on organizational change. Such differences exist not only across academic persuasions but also within each one of them. On the one hand, such differences are indicative of the complexity and multidimensionality of the phenomenon. On the other , they suggest the need to search for a more integrative and synthetic approach.

Such a synthesis is recently emerging in the literature. In the area of business policy, authors such as Mintzberg (1978) and Burgelman (1983) have suggested that a firm's strategy has both an induced and an autonomous component. The former, shaped by the existing structural context, leads to change that is incremental and evolutionary, and the latter, driven by entrepreneurial potential that may exist at any level of the management hierarchy, can lead to changes that we have characterized as strategic leaps. In a subsequent extension of the concept, Burgelman (1985) has attempted to reconcile the rational and natural selection views, arguing that the relative strengths of the induced and autonomous components of strategy depend on the state of the environment and the internal context of the firm. In effect, the argument is that both kinds of changes are feasible and can be obtained under different conditions.

Another integrative perspective is that of Lawrence and Dyer (1983). These authors have suggested that the readaptive capacity of an organization depends on the nature and extent of environmental uncertainties. In particular, they consider two kinds of environmental uncertainties to be critical. First is resource scarcity (RS), which is a composite measure of the availability to the organization of all its essential resorces. The second is information complexity (IC), which is defined as the "degree of competitive, product, market, technological, and regulatory variations in a firm's relevant environment" (300). Using a framwork in which IC and RS form two dimensions of a grid, Lawrence and Dyer have shown how the different concepts and findings about organizational change can all be true under different environmental and organizational contexts. A firm's readaptive capacity, according to these authors, is highest when both IC and RS are at moderate levels and reduces when either of them becomes too high or too low.

IMPLICATIONS FOR STRATEGIC CONTROL

These integrative and contingency-oriented perspectives on organizational change are central to the concept of strategic control that we present in this book. We find the arguments of Burgelman and Lawrence and Dyer compelling, and this is reflected in our discussions in this and the following chapters. If one adopts a totally "rational actor" perspective, strategic control is indistinguishable from strategy implementation, since organizational change can be created by implementing a set of strategies that bridge the gap between the current and the desired state of the firm. In contrast, if one accepts the world view of the population ecologists, the concept of strategic control becomes meaningless, since managers are considered incapable of proactively influencing the process of organizational change. If change is only evolutionary, the notion of strategic leaps becomes infeasible, just as if change is only revolutionary, incremental adjustment of positon through managing existing momentum no longer remains valid.

The eclectic perspectives of Burgelman and Lawrence and Dyer consider each of these views as valid under certain conditions. A corollary that follows is that managers can influence the nature and extent of change if they can influence those conditions. That view is precisely what we are advocating: Strategic control is the process of managing organizational change by influencing the variables that determine the contingency conditions. All the variables need not be susceptible to managerial influence. All that is required is that managers should be able to affect some of them, at least at the margin. Our objective in this book is to identify some of the variables that can be affected and to suggest how they can be used as leverage points to create organizational change—either incrementally or through discrete jumps.

ORGANIZATIONAL ADAPTATION: A FIRST CUT

Adaptation and Organizational Learning

Cyert and March (1963), Terreberry (1968), and March and Olsen (1976) are among those who have argued that adaptive organizations are those in which members have the capacity to learn to predict changes in their environments, search for alternative sources of sustenance, and develop and maintain a mechanism for storing information about possible interchangeable input-output components. Drawing fom this proposition, Duncan and Weiss (1978) have defined organizational learning as "that process in the organization through which members of the dominant coalition develop, over time, the ability to discover when organizational changes are required and what changes can be undertaken which they believe will succeed" (78). Learning is therefore an essential prerequisite for organizations to adapt. Adaptive organizations are those that have capabilities to learn.

Argyris and Schon (1981) distinguish among three different kinds of organizational learning: single loop, double loop and deutero. In single loop learning, "members of the organization respond to changes in the internal and external environments of the organization by detecting errors which they then correct so as to maintain the central feature of the organizational theory-in-use. . . . [In such learning] there is a single feedback loop which connects detected outcomes of action to organizational strategies and assumptions which are modified so as to keep organizational performance within the range set by organizational norms. The norms themselves—for product quality, sales or task performance—remain unchanged" (18–19). In double loop learning, on the other hand, "there is . . . a double feedback loop which connects the detection of error not only to strategies and assumptions for effective performance but to the very norms which define effective performance" (22). Finally, deutero learning is a still higher level learning process whereby the organization learns how to learn.

Any process of control involves a process of learning. However, single loop learning, as defined by Argyris and Schon, primarily takes place in the domain of what we have labeled tactical control. Double loop and deutero learning—learning where the basic assumptions and norms are themselves made open to questions and change—is the principal objective of strategic control. This distinction is somewhat fuzzy, for as Argyris and Schon themselves point out, "the distinction between single and double loop learning is less a binary one than might first appear" (25). The basic point is that in tactical control, the focal question is whether the organization is achieving its objectives. In strategic control, the correctness of the objectives themselves is subjected to questioning.

We adopt the unfreeze-change-refreeze framework to model the process of organizational adaptation inherent in our concept of strategic control. No learning takes place in a vacuum, and a process of unlearning may have to precede any process of learning (Hedberg, Nystrom, and Starbuck 1976). We, however, prefer the term *sensitizing* to *unfreezing* since it suggests that the impetus for unlearning arises from sensitivity to changes in the key variables. Sensitizing leads to learning, which, as suggested by Daft and Weick (1984), includes the concept of action. Learning includes actual adaptive actions that are triggered by it. Finally, the learning is *institutionalized*—a term we prefer to *refreezing*—thereby setting up a new set of dynamics that move the organization forward (see Figure 2.1).

Sensitizing

In the organizational development literature, the impetus for change arises from disconfirmation of present behavior or attitude. Such disconfirmation can be due to any number of reasons, and it

Figure 2.1   The Adaptation Process

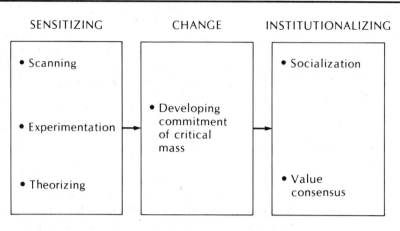

causes discomfort that initiates the change process (Schein 1980). The discomfort must, however, be sufficient to motivate a change, for if discomfort or anxiety is at a low level, it can easily be dealt with by denial or problem avoidance. This role of a problem or of a "goal performance mismatch" in initiating a change has been noted by many researchers (e.g., Beckhard and Harris 1977; Galbraith and Nathanson 1978). Thus, the unfreezing process is relatively simple when an organization passes through a serious crisis like a dramatic fall in growth or profitability. But it is much more difficult in the absence of such a crisis, because the desire and preference for the status quo either for internal political reasons (Pfeffer 1978) or arising out of uncertainty avoidance behavior (Cyert and March 1963) dominate the desire for change. Thus, a critical problem for strategic control is how to create an environment that will allow unfreezing even in the absence of cataclysmic events.

Another issue of concern in this regard is the distinction between symptoms and the problem. Usually visible is not the problem but the symptom—a fall in market share or a delay in deliveries, for instance. The problem has to be found (Pounds 1965) or formulated by analyzing the symptoms. The same symptom—say, failure in meeting supply commitments—may arise from different problems such as general expansion of demand in excess of capacity or poor maintenance of equipment leading to increased and erratic downtimes, and may therefore require different corrective actions. Schein (1969) models problem formulation as an analytical process of generalization based on the experience of critical incidents (see Figure 2.2).

Figure 2.2   Steps in Problem Formulation (From Schein 1969)

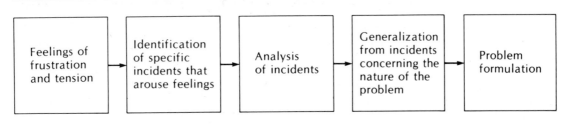

Edgar Schein, PROCESS CONSULTATION, © 1969, Addison-Wesley, Reading, Massachusetts. Pg. 49, Fig. 5.2. Reprinted with permission.

These steps of analysis and generalization are key to the concept of strategic control. As Pounds argues, such generalization is possible only when managers have a mental model of how things work, a map, and a schema—a theory of action, in the learning theory terminology of Argyris and Schon. However, where the concept of strategic control goes beyond the problem-finding process of Pounds is that now the model or the theory of action itself comes within the purview of the questioning process.

Our concept of sensitizing, as mentioned earlier, is based on but goes beyond by concept of unfreezing. First, it is endogenous, to be achieved internally, within the organization, as a continuous function, and not through the discrete efforts of an external consultant. Second, it operates even at normal times without the dubious benefit of a crisis. Third, it includes sensitivity not only to the key variables but also to the assumptions that underlie the process of identifying the key variables. Finally, sensitizing is in large measure a function of the individual values that make up the corporate culture; it is a matter of individual internalized beliefs as well as a group consensus on the need for certain kinds of change.

Let us illustrate this concept of sensitizing with a specific example[1]. Between 1980 and 1984, the Coca Cola Company (Coke) has undergone a major transition that has often been referred to as a cultural revolution (see, for instance, the Wall Street Journal, June 29, 1984, p. 6). In 1980, Coke appeared to be a cornered defender, gradually losing its position to Pepsico (Pepsi), its archrival in the soft drink business. There was no crisis, but a gradual decline. The company had allowed Pepsi to slowly move ahead of it in the important category of U.S. supermarket sales. The U.S. market share of its flagship product—brand Coke— had dropped gradually from 26.6

---

[1]We are grateful to Stephen Leichtman for providing this example.

percent in 1977 to 24.3 percent in 1980. Simultaneously, brand Pepsi had increased its share from 17.2 to 17.9 percent (These narrow movements do not appear significant till one is reminded that each share point represents approximately $200 million in retail sales). The company's overall share in the U.S. soft drink market had decreased from 35.3 to 34.4 percent in the 1975–1980 period, while Pepsico's total share had moved up from 20.8 to 24.4 percent. Internationally too, Pepsico had become the aggressor and had overtaken Coke in a few markets including Venezuela and the Philippines.

By the end of 1984, the situation had been substantially reversed. Coke's share of the U.S. soft drink market had increased to 36.4 percent. It had launched a new product—diet Coke—that was acclaimed as "very likely the most successful new product introduction ever" (Marketing and Media Decision, April, 1984). It had significantly improved its profitability by selling off some operations (Tenco and Aqua-Chem), acquiring new businesses (Columbia Pictures) and putting renewed emphasis on others (Minute Maid orange juice). Internationally, it had increased its lead over Pepsico and its net income per share had soared from $3.27 in 1980 to $4.76 in 1984, while Pepsi's dipped from $2.86 to $2.25 over the same period. In early 1985, Fortune magazine, based on a survey of U.S. business executives, listed Coke at the second most admired company in the country (Fortune, Jan. 7, 1985, p. 67).

Most analysts ascribe this dramatic turn-around in Coke to the youthful dynamism of its new CEO—Roberto C. Goizueta—a Cuban immigrant who, before taking over the stewardship of the company, had only two years of upper management experience and that too in Coke's Aqua Chem boiler building subsidiary. Essentially what Goizueta did was to unfreeze a set of assumptions that, unchallenged over decades, had become sacred cows of the company.

One such assumption was that the name 'Coke' can never be used in another brand. Established by Robert W. Woodruff, the person who made Coke a household name around the globe, this assumption was the most sacred of all the sacred cows in Coke. Goizueta brought this assumption out in the open, made it debatable, and the result was diet Coke. While many factors combined to make diet Coke as resounding a success as it turned out to be, it is clear that the "Coke" name was a major asset for the brand that gave it a great advantage over other diet soft drinks, including its own lackluster half-brother, Tab.

Another such deeprooted assumption in Coke was that bottling was not Coke's business and it must follow an arm's length policy with regard to its world-wide network of independent bottlers. The management style of Goizueta helped in making this assumption explicit, and therefore open to questioning. This mental jump, in turn, made it clear to company managers that the local bottlers were the key instruments for Coke to leverage its own marketing competence. It also made the managers sensitive to the fact that decades of hands off policy had led to gradual atrophying of the entrepreneurial spirit in the bottling companies and had significantly weakened a key strategic asset of the company.

The result of this awareness was a major new strategic thrust that led to a thorough overhaul of Coke's bottlers all over the world. The Company bought out all poor performing units and resold them to well financed, well managed organizations who were interested in "intelligent risk taking, and no holds barred marketing" (Leichtman, 1985). This strategy was carried out throughout the United States and in a number of countries around the world including Canada, Germany, Greece, Philippines, Venezuela and the United Kingdom. To do so, Coke had to change another time honoured tradition—that debt must be avoided as far as possible—and borrow large sums in the capital market. The program has so far caused approximately 50 percent of Coke's bottling capacity to change hands, with a total transaction value of over $2.5 billion. Besides changing bottlers, Coke has also increased their territories in many cases so as to let them take advantage of economies of scale. The resulting cost savings have allowed the bottlers to increase pressure on competitors—often Pepsi—through price reduction.

As this example of Coke illustrates, unfreezing of old assumptions is often a prerequisite for strategic change. However, it is rarely sufficient for change or learning to actually occur. For that, the organization requires three other attributes. First, it must acquire external information to understand what changes are required. Second, it must possess required resources to search for alternatives and to formulate its responses to the environmental stimuli. Finally, it must have an internal value system that reduces resistance to change among members of the firm.

Information: Detailed and accurate information on internal and external environments does not guarantee sensitivity but its absence is a sufficient condition to prevent it. Sensitizing a firm requires the installation of an effective and ongoing mechanism for acquiring environmental stimuli by monitoring key variables such as economic, technological and regulatory conditions, relative competitive position, and any emerging issues as perceived by key players in the organization. It also requires an internal information system for monitoring progress on all strategic programs as well as specific indicators of concern such as product quality, costs, employee skill levels, and morale.

Duncan and Weiss (1978) have identified three mechanisms

through which organizations acquire information and knowledge. First and perhaps the most important is scanning. Such scanning is carried out by the organization both informally, with members acquiring information in the routine course of their work, and formally through dedicated units engaged in competitor analysis, technology monitoring, political risk analysis, and other such specialized activities. In the following chapter, we shall discuss the topic of scanning in considerable detail and shall review how this mechanism can be used as a leverage point in the strategic control systems of the firm.

An organization can also accumulate information by engaging in experimental actions (i.e., through trial and error). The results of such experiments constitute a repertoire of action-outcome knowledge. Various patterns may be observed and they, too, become a part of the organization's knowledge pool. This rationale lies behind the "Ready-Fire-Aim" sequence suggested by Peters and Waterman (1982) as one characteristic of excellent companies.

Finally, an organization can also increase knowledge by armchair theorizing. Individuals within the organization may formulate new action outcome relationships or detect flaws in existing ones through inductive or deductive analysis. Theory (such as input-output analysis or industrial organizational theory) or intuition may be the source of such knowledge.

Resources: To acquire and process external information through scanning, experimentation or theorizing, and organization requires slack resources. Extreme scarcity of resources results in reduction of these activities and in a gradual reduction in the organization's sensitivity to external change.

However, abundance of slack resources also has the opposite effect on breeding contentment and limiting the range of problemistic search (Cyert and March, 1963). Excessive slack can lead to reduction in the organization's attention to external change and in strengthening internal forces of resistance to change (Starbuck and Hedberg, 1977; Hedberg, 1981). Williamson (1964) has demonstrated the corollary that diminishing resources increases an organization's willingness to change.

Slack resources, therefore, create the organizational dilemma that they promote the ability to change at the cost of willingness to change (Hedberg, 1981; Bourgeois, 1981). One solution to this problem is the creation of two different kinds of resources in an organization: a normal operational resource pool and a strategic resource pool. The level of scarcity in the normal operative resources can be managed in a way that keeps a tight control on slack and thereby avoids strategic stagnation that arises out of affluence. Yet, sufficient slack can be maintained in the strategic pool to permit search, experimentation, learning, and building up a knowledge base for facilitating change. The "two-hat" system at Texas Instruments is an example of such a dual system in operation. Managers in this company control two separate budgets: one strategic and the other operational. They wear two different hats in allocating expenses out of these budgets. The strategic budget is used to create and maintain long-term effectiveness of the firm, while the operational budget is tightly controlled to achieve short-term efficiency (see Lorange and Vancil 1977 for a detailed description).

Reducing Resistance to Change. Commitment and perseverance are among the prime virtues that most organizations tend to promote, primarily through an internal value system that implicitly or explicitly rewards such behavior. Yet, as argued by Staw (1982), these are precisely the factors that create and strengthen resistance to change. They entrap individuals and groups to continued commitment to a course of action, often beyond the point where benefits exceed costs.

Another source of resistance to change, one that is intertwined with and inseparable from the organizational value system, is the internal power dynamics. As March and Simon (1958) suggest, an existing system is created by those in power and presumably serves their interests. Change has the potential for disrupting not only the distribution of power but also the mechanisms and norms that determine the distribution process. Thus, strategic change will likely be resisted by those in power.

A direct coupling of power with short-term performance only makes the position worse. Such a linkage reduces the "psychological safety" (Schein 1980) that is essential for developing organizational willingness for change. Decoupling the two, or more pragmatically, maintaining a loose coupling between them, helps create an environment in which admission of error and motivation for change become easier. Another mechanism for reducing resistance to change is to separate status, power, and influence within the organization. As Bacharach and Lawler (1980) point out, power is indivisible but influence is not, and an organizational system can be built where status neither requires nor generates power, influence is distributed widely based on knowledge and involvement, and power is controlled through a consensual process. Although such systems are typically associated with the Japanese style of management, *In Search of Excellence* shows their feasibility for U.S. firms.

Thus, sensitivity to change can be enhanced in an organization through changes in management processes such as those of scanning and experimentation, and also through manipulation of structural attributes that determine internal distribution and assignment of status, power, and influence. It can also be enhanced through resource allocation mechanisms by maintaining slack resources for strategic activities and by avoiding slack at the normal operative level.

Change

In the social psychology–based OD literature, the source of the unfreeze-change-refreeze model, change is seen as a discrete, stop-go process. An organization, like any social system, seeks stability. Thus, over time it freezes a set of assumptions, values, norms, and artifacts through accumulation of reinforcements. In such a scheme, the frozen pattern gradually falls out of step with reality, requiring the implementation of the process of unfreezing the existing state, injecting the change, and refreezing it again to achieve stability. Change, in this model, is viewed as a surgical process.

We, on the other hand, view organizational change as a continuous process wherein the strategic control mechanism keeps the organization in a permanent state of sensitivity—in a semifluid condition, so to speak. Thus, the step of injecting or introducing change is no longer a separate part of the process. Instead, we see change as arising from a continuous process of learning. Through information acquisition, experimentation, and theorizing, the process of sensitizing enhances the level of organizational intelligence and thereby facilitates the overall ability of the organization to create and implement change.

However, a specific act of change requires that a critical mass of the organization's members must be on board. The critical mass consists of the smallest number of key actors involved in implementing the change.

The overall feasibility of the change depends on two attributes of the members of the critical mass: their readiness for the change and their capability for making it happen[1]. Thus, for a particular change situation, the critical mass may consist of three actors: X1, X2, X3, and their readiness and capability may be as shown in Table 2.1.

Members in the critical mass may therefore have different levels of commitment to the change, with different perspectives that may be related but not overlapping. They may be categorized as

---

[1]This model was suggested by Richard Beckhard to one of the authors who was his student at the Sloan School of Management, MIT.

Table 2.1 Critical Mass Analysis

Critical Mass Members	Readiness for Change	Capability to Create Change
X1	Low	High
X2	Medium	Low
X3	Low	Medium

- those who would *let* it happen,
- those who would *help* it happen, and
- those who would *make* it happen.

How the actual change can come about is illustrated by Figure 2.3. The *O*'s represent the current state of commitments of the three actors. However, to make the change happen, X1 must be fully committed (i.e., must feel that she must make it happen). X3 must actively help it happen, while X2 must not hinder it (i.e., must let it happen). That is the minimum configuration for the change to be implemented. Thus, the first step in executing the change, in Beckhard's scheme, is to move X1 to the "make it happen" state and X3 to the "help it happen" state (shown by *X*'s in Figure 2.3). Nothing needs to be done with X2, for his state of commitment is already higher than the minimum required of him.

This model is the one we use, but with a different perspective. Strategic change is endogenous, not triggered by a specific change agent (or consultant, as in Beckhard's model). We take the concept of capability and use it as weights (i.e., as a controllable variable for

Figure 2.3 *The Process of Creating Change*

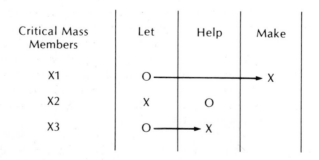

the management). Weights can be changed formally (by firing or promoting) or informally, through status-creating mechanisms. The commitment states can be changed through scanning, experimenting, communicating, and learning. Finally, the states of commitments are dependent on the nature and extent of the change. If the extent is made smaller, some in the "let" category will move to the "help" category, and so on. The extent of change, then, is another controllable variable. Change can therefore be influenced endogenously through manipulation of any of the three variables—that is, the weights assigned to individuals, the sensitizing mechanisms, and the extent of change being sought. Out of them, manipulating the sensitizing mechanisms is a long-term process, which we have already discussed briefly. The other two leverage points (i.e., changing the levels of influence exerted by individual managers and adjusting the nature and extent of change attempted) have a stronger short-term effect on the organization's ability to achieve change.

Let us first consider the issue of individual influence. If a certain change is considered desirable, and if it is known that particular individuals are strongly in favor of such changes, the probability of implementing the change would increase to the extent that the status, power, or influence of those individuals increases. Stated differently, this is the concept of empowering champions described by both Peters and Waterman (1982) and Kanter (1983). Similarly, if CEOs are considered the principal agents to create change, assigning them a high level of status and power can tip the balance in favor of change, irrespective of the commitment levels of other organizational members. This has been satirically referred to as the "John Wayne style of management," but it can be appropriate under certain organizational contexts—perhaps in managing a difficult turnaround. To some extent, this model is inherent in the rationalist version of strategy proposed by authors such as Andrews (1980).

Altering the extent of change (i.e., the gap between the current and the proposed states) is the other control variable suggested by the model. By making this gap small, opposing forces can be reduced and adequate support at the "let it happen" state can achieve the small change desired. This scheme is behind the model of logical incrementalism proposed by Quinn (1980). In our framework, this approach is most suitable when the environment is relatively stable and continuous (i.e., during peacetime). Under such conditions, gradual repositioning of the firm is managed by delicate control of momentum so that change is achieved incrementally, in small steps, without upsetting the apple cart. Such an approach is feasible, since external change is also incremental. It would not do, however, when external change is turbulent. Under such conditions, strategic leaps may be required. This is facilitated, on the long term, by widespread sensitizing and communication that creates greater homogeneity within the critical mass and enhances the commitment states of a larger number of organizational members. Such homogeneity and enhanced sensitivity permit widening the gap between the present and the proposed states while retaining the benefits of incrementalism. In the short run, strategic leaps can also be facilitated by an appropriate redistribution of power and influence (i.e., by creating, legitimizing, and empowering internal champions and change agents). The reward and punishment system in the organization as well as its overall culture and values are critical in this regard. These issues are of immense practical importance in operationalizing and implementing strategic control, and we discuss them in greater detail in Chapters 5, 6, and 7.

INSTITUTIONALIZATION

Most authors have conceptualized institutionalization largely as a rule-making process. A definition proposed by Meyer and Rowan (1977) is typical: "Institutionalization involves the process by which social processes, obligations or actualities come to take on a rule-like status in social thought and action" (341). Institutionalization, from this perspective, "deals with persistence or perpetuation of activities. . . . Institutionalized acts are done for no reason other than that is how things are done" (Pfeffer 1982).

Such a definition arises because the authors examine institutionalization in terms of specific acts or behaviors of organizational members. An act is perceived as institutionalized when it is performed by multiple individuals given a common stimulus, when it persists over time, and when such behavior exists external to any individual (Goodman, Bazerman, and Conlon 1979). Given this definition, the process of institutionalization, as viewed by these authors, bears a close resemblance to Weber's description of how a bureaucratic organization functions.

Selznick (1957) proposes a different view of institutionalization—a view that we share. Institutionalization, according to him, is the infusion of values into an organization that would impart to it a permanence that extends beyond its current objectives. It means more than common behavior; it is the creation of a common purpose.

Institutionalization, in our framework, is the diffusion of organizational learning so that it becomes a part of the organization's assumptions and values. Through institutionalization, a change is stabilized and internalized within the firm. Institutionalization is the creation of a social fact (Goodman and Dean 1982), but it is also the creation of a shared context that gives the fact a meaning.

Goodman and Dean (1982) have identified a number of factors that facilitate institutionalization. Out of them, we consider two to be of primary importance:

1. *Socialization.* Socialization refers to processes through which information about beliefs, preferences, norms, and values is transmitted to organizational members. Socialization increases commitment to organizational objectives and facilitates common adoption of change, at least on a trial basis.

2. *Normative and Value Consensus.* The second factor is closely related to and follows from the concept of socialization. It is the extent of homogeneity of beliefs and goals that exists in the organization and is of particular importance to the continuance of a changed assumption or response.

The primary reasons why a change is often not stabilized is that it does not fit the internal structures, systems, norms, and assumptions of the organization or because it does not fit the realities of the organization's environment or expectations of the external stakeholders.

Often, the misfit arises not because the change itself is inappropriate (though that can also happen) but because all linked systems are not changed, thus creating bottlenecks that initiate the rejection mechanism. This is particularly true of large and complex organizations where a strategic change affects a complicated web of related subsystems, each of which must be adapted to the change. For instance, a change from growth through acquisition to growth through internal development calls for changes not only in the R&D establishment but also in marketing strategies and in personnel planning. For any change to be effective, all such implications need to be carefully analyzed to prevent the total system from going out of sync.

This problem is particularly acute for the diversified organizations. These organizations often have quite different norms and cultures in different divisions (even more so if the firm has followed a strategy of growth through acquisitions). In addition, the divisions are usually linked to each other and to the corporate office through complex systems of vertical and horizontal relationships. In such organizations, tracing through the effect of a strategic change at the corporate level may quickly get out of hand. In such circumstances, an organized process of diffusion is essential for any strategic change to be effective.

Institutionalization in the sense of a system for diffusion is considerably easier if the change is brought about through a process of strategic control rather than as a one-time surgical measure. Strategic control initiates change on the basis of why the change is required, not just what is to be changed. Widespread diffusion of the "why" permits a decentralized approach to the related changes. In the more traditional top-down approach to change, the "what is to be changed" is communicated. In the absence of an understanding of the reasons for change, subunits find it difficult to anticipate changes required at their level. At the same time, the complexities of the subunit systems can rarely be fully understood at the corporate level. Thus, neither can clearly see the implications of the change, thereby creating the potential for inconsistencies and a possible demand for reverting to the old and familiar state.

The institutionalization process also provides a sense of stability in the organization. We have viewed the change process as arising out of a continuous sensitivity to changing key variables, which creates an environment of openness to change. But no social system can survive without some stability; it is essential for the psychology of its members. Institutionalization provides this stability. In our model, openness to change is continuous, but change itself, particularly at the strategic level, is not. One of the advantages of strategic control is that it avoids the physical and psychological waste of the trial and error process of change—the "muddling through" process documented by Lindbloom (1959) and others. Strategic control leads to well-formulated change, which can therefore remain stable while it anticipates the future as much as it extrapolates from the past.

Thus, our model of change, to quote Peters and Waterman (1982) a little out of context, has simultaneous loose-tight properties. It maintains a permanent tension in the organizational system through sensitizing, it permits changes in response to environmental shifts before they accumulate to the level of crisis, and it diffuses and stabilizes the change to prepare the system for the next wave.

3

Leverage Points for Managing the Process of Strategic Control

The basic premise of this book is that strategic control is necessary for more effective alignment of the organization with the characteristics and demands of its environment. The nature of the environment is what drives the process of strategic control. Further, we have stressed that a primary objective of strategic control is to facilitate organizational learning. Such learning drives the organization forward through the exigencies of the external world.

In Chapter 2, we presented a model of the strategic adaptation process. In this chapter, we review the interactions between this process and the nature of the external environment. In the course of our arguments, we make three main points. First, we argue that *perceived* characteristics of the external environment drive the organizational adaptation process. We suggest that the members' perceptions about the environment, rather than any objective reality, is of importance in understanding the environmental impact on adaptation.

Second, we suggest that perceptions about the environment are influenced by a set of organizational filters. The structure of the organization, the information systems, and the extent of slack available within the organization are some of the filters that affect how the organization will perceive the environment.

Finally, we argue that this view of the organizational adaptation process is useful, since it suggests some of the leverage points through which managers can influence the adaptive capabilities of their firms. A principal component of strategic control is managing these leverage points so as to enhance the organization's ability to learn from the environment and to self-design change to maintain its equilibrium. We identify these leverage points and conclude the chapter with a brief discussion of how managerial actions might influence these leverage points and therefore achieve the objectives of strategic control.

ENACTING ENVIRONMENTS: THE ROLE OF ORGANIZATIONAL FILTERS

The Enacted Environment

Every organization faces a real objective environment, or rather many real objective environments, which are determined by attributes of its input, throughput, and output processes—the nature of its customers and the structure of its competition, the availability of its raw materials and other inputs, the demands of the government, and the expectations of the people in the community within which it exists. These are or are caused by tangible things—they can be kicked and can, from time to time, kick back. They impose real demands on the organization and bestow real benefits to those that meet those demands and equally real punishments on those that do not. This is the real world that businesspeople and managers must deal with, and the organization must try to identify the attributes of this real objective environment as inputs to its adaptation process. However, like the uncertainty principle in physics, the very process of observation affects the outcome. Since environments are perceived by organizations or, more accurately, by individuals within the organization, the perception is influenced by who the individuals are and what they represent; what you see depends on where you stand. At the individual level, the perception is affected by the objectives, agenda, and role of the person. At the organizational level, it is influenced by the overall structure of roles, the way the organization is integrated and differentiated (Lawrence and Lorsch 1967), and the extent of its internal slack. Dill (1958) emphasized this subjective aspect of the environment—subjective because both the perception and the interpretation processes are influenced by a priori theories and beliefs (Starbuck 1976). Weick (1969) has called it the process of enactment, both in the sense of a decree, as by a legislative process, and in the form of reconstruction, as in staging a play (Pfeffer and Salancik 1978).

Attributes of the Environment

The environment is perceived by the concerned actors as a sum total of a diverse range of disjointed signals. To treat it analytically, one needs a construct or categorization scheme, just as managers must find a way of integrating environmental signals into a meaningful picture. Many such categorization schemes have been proposed in the literature, from simple two stages of heterogeneity and stability (Lawrence and Lorsch 1967; Thompson 1967) to a complex sixteen-by-four matrix (Jurkovich 1974). Arguments about the appropriateness of categorization have been based on both construct validity and measurement accuracy (Tosi, Aldag, and Storey 1972), and as yet no consensus has been reached on how to either conceptualize or operationalize environmental attributes.

For this discussion, we adopt a simple scheme that is neither original nor exhaustive but adequate for our purposes. We consider the environment to have two broad dimensions: one of *complexity* and the other of *munificence* (see Figure 3.1).

The complexity of the environment is determined by two factors: *heterogeneity* or number of environmental components and the degree of similarity or differences between them (Duncan 1972), and *dynamism*, which is determined both by the rate of change and by the stability of that rate (Child 1972; Aldrich 1979). Environmental munificence reflects the amount of slack available in the organization's environment and depends on two factors: the overall availability of resources required for the organization to survive and the extent of demands placed on those resources by competing organizations.

Figure 3.1   Attributes of the Environment

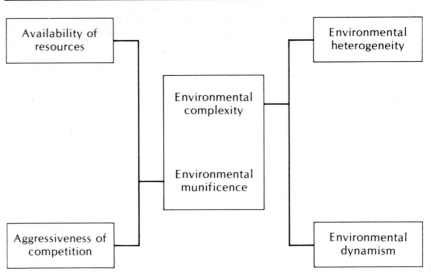

The Enactment Process: Role of Organizational Filters

As discussed earlier, environmental attributes, as perceived or enacted by the actors, are influenced by different individual and organizational factors. These factors determine both what aspects of the environment will be given attention and also how the selected components will be perceived. They act as filters through which the objective environment is perceived by organizational members.

How complex the environment is perceived to be depends not only on the objective attributes of heterogeneity and stability but also on the organizational structure, the configuration of roles, and the internal information systems (see Figure 3.2). If a company has a separate customer complaint department reporting directly to top management, the needs and problems of customers will be perceived within the organization differently than if the function is a part of the marketing or production department. Complexity of the competitive environment will be seen differently if a separate cell exists for competitive analysis compared with when the function is not as specifically differentiated. Even if the function is differentiated, the perception will be different depending on whether it is a permanent group under the planning department or a quasi-temporary team including representatives from sales, production, planning, and R&D.

Finally, if internal reporting systems require information only on

Figure 3.2 Environmental Complexity: Mediating Organizational Filters of Structure, Role Configuration, and Information Systems

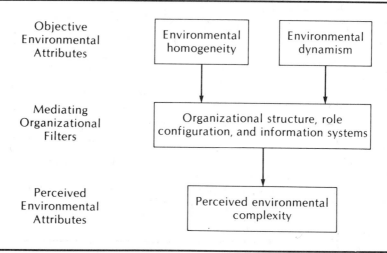

| Objective Environmental Attributes | Environmental homogeneity | Environmental dynamism |

| Mediating Organizational Filters | Organizational structure, role configuration, and information systems |

| Perceived Environmental Attributes | Perceived environmental complexity |

current products and performance, attention to the environment will be domain focused. If, instead, the internal information systems explicitly require inputs about broader socioeconomic issues, scanning will be more broad based and diverse, again leading to different perceptions about the complexity of the environment.

Perceived environmental munificence is similarly influenced by the extent of organizational slack (see Figure 3.3). The term *slack*, however, needs some elaboration, since it has been used by different authors in many different senses (see Bourgeois 1981 for a comprehensive and creative review).

Organizational slack refers to the cushion of actual or potential resources available to the organization in excess of the minimum required to meet its current obligations. It is the extent of uncommitted resources that an organization possesses (Cyert and March 1963).

As argued by Simon (1957) and March and Simon (1958), organizational slack can diminish attention to the environment: It can exacerbate "satisfying" behavior and limit search. It can mute the warning signals of an environmental threat. A history of past successes, large and visible surplus funds, or surging revenues from a soon-to-die cash cow can all diminish the sense of competitive intensity and drying resources, as can surplus layers of personnel and a system of ceremonial and expensive rituals continuing from a past era of affluence.

Figure 3.3 Environmental Munificence: Mediating Filter Organizational Slack

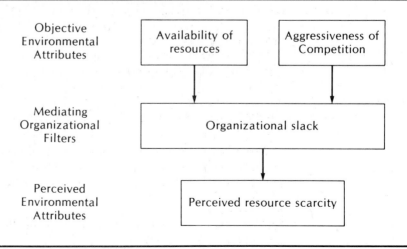

However, as suggested in Chapter 2, slack can also promote creative strategic behavior. It can provide resources for innovation—for introducing new products and entering new markets—and for taking bold risks (see Hambrick and Snow 1977 and Bourgeois 1981).

Slack can therefore produce both innovative and suboptimal strategic behavior, but overall it tends to act as a buffer between the organization and the environment and to dull the organization's sensitivity to environmental variances and discontinuities (Thompson 1967).

PERCEIVED ENVIRONMENT
AND ORGANIZATIONAL ADAPTATION

Lawrence and Dyer (1983) have suggested how the organizational adaptive (in their language, readaptive) capabilities are most effective when both environmental (or information) complexity and resource scarcity are at moderate levels. We have argued previously that organizational perceptions about both these environmental characteristics are mediated by a set of organizational filters. In other words, we do not see either as something fixed and beyond the control of the organization, though in an objective sense, they are. What is important is that managers can at least partially control the perceptions of complexity and scarcity by manipulating organizational filters and thereby modify the organization's capacity for readaptation.[1]

Chapter 2 described a simple model of the organizational adaptation process. It was a partial analyis in which the effects of environmental characteristics on adaptation mechanisms was not considered. As suggested earlier in this chapter, we view the adaptation process as driven by the organization's perception of the environment. These perceptions are derived from the objective environment but are also different because of selective attention and reconstruction due to the effect of organizational filters such as structure, information systems, culture, and slack. A more complete schematic representation of our views on the adaptation process in shown in Figure 3.4. Adaptation takes place through the sequential processes of sensitizing, change, and institutionalization. The whole process takes place within the bounds of an organizational context. This context affects both purely internal processes, but more important to our purposes, it acts as a filter through

---

[1]We are indebted to Prof. Howard Stevenson of The Harvard Business School for suggesting this idea.

Figure 3.4   _Environmental Influence on Organizational Adaptation_

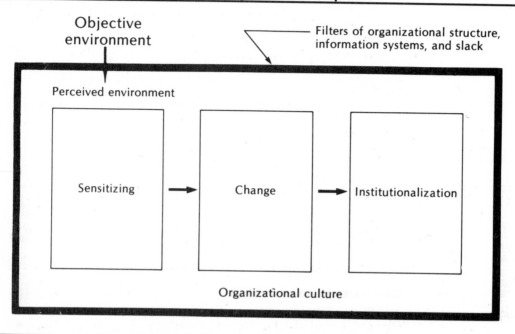

which the external environment is perceived. The following paragraphs describe how such perceptions may affect the sensitizing and learning processes in organizations.

Sensitizing

As we discussed in Chapter 2, information about the environment is received by the organization through scanning and through experimentation. Daft and Weick (1984) have recently proposed a model of the organization as an interpretation system and have suggested that organizations adopt different scanning mechanisms depending on their perceptions about the analyzability of the environment and the extent of their own intrusiveness into the environment (see Figure 3.5). When organizations perceive the environment as analyzable but are passive themselves in their efforts to analyze, relying on whatever information the environment gives them, their dominant scanning mechanism is what Aguilar (1967) called _conditioned viewing._

Figure 3.5   Scanning Modes (From Daft and Weick 1984)

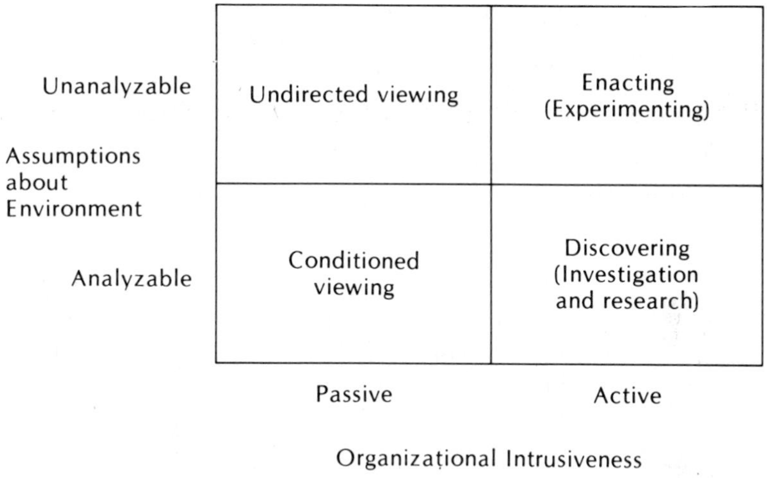

	Passive	Active
Unanalyzable	Undirected viewing	Enacting (Experimenting)
Analyzable	Conditioned viewing	Discovering (Investigation and research)

Assumptions about Environment

Organizational Intrusiveness

They tend to rely on established data collection procedures and interpretations developed within traditional boundaries. The environment is perceived as objective and benevolent, so the organization does not take unusual steps to learn about the environment. The viewing is conditioned in the sense that it is limited to routine documents, reports, publications, and information systems that have grown up through the years. (Daft and Weick 1984, 289)

Undirected viewing was defined by Aguilar as keeping in touch with the environment through oriented exposure to information that might be useful. It is a little more focused than random or even general curiosity but less directed than conditioned viewing. The undirected viewing mode is adopted by passive organizations when they assume the environment to be unanalyzable. "Managers act on limited, soft information" and are "open to cues about the environment from many sources" (Daft and Weick 1984).

When the environment is seen as analyzable, the active organization adopts the *discovering* mode, which involves formal investigation and search to detect the correct nature of the environment. The organization uses market research, trend analysis, and other forecasting techniques to predict problems and opportunities.

Finally, the active organization confronting an environment that it considers unanalyzable adopts the *enacting* mode where experimentation, testing, simulation, and trial and error are given priority over analysis. "An organization in this mode tends to construct markets rather than waiting for an assessment of demand to tell it what to produce" (Daft and Weick 1984, 289).

The strategic control dimension of the model emerges if we turn it inside out. In a complex (unanalyzable) environment, the active organization proactively experiments; the passive organization reactively views. What happens, then, if in a complex environment, the management of an organization actively promotes experimentation—induces the hands-on–value-driven culture so picturesquely described by Peters and Waterman (1982)? Does the organization tend to become more active? Does it shift from being a reactor to being a prospector? In organizational dynamics, causation is rarely, if ever, unidirectional. Thus, if scanning behavior reflects organizational orientation, it molds it just as much. We propose that specific scanning modes do much more than collect external information—in the long term, they act as instruments for strategic change and as agents for sensitizing.

Learning

The process of learning is influenced by the same factors that influence the choice of information acquisition modes: the perceived complexity (and hence, analyzability) of the environment and the intrusiveness or proactiveness of the firm. When the environment is seen as analyzable, it is essentially seen as continuous. This, in our terminology, leads to the momentum management mode. The learning process, in this mode, involves many rules for assembling the interpretation (Weick 1969), many techniques, much planning, and a formalized system for tactical and operational control. When, however, the environment is seen as discontinuous (nonanalyzable), the assembly rules are few: Equivocality reduction is achieved through consultation or through taking action and seeing what works (Weick 1969; Daft and Weick 1984). Compare Matsushita's simultaneous introduction of many models to see which the customers accept with Procter and Gamble's enormous research and analysis to identify every perceivable detail of a new product, which is then launched with full commitment of resources.

The learning process is also influenced greatly by the culture of the organization. The capacity of humans to resist learning is phenomenal. In a highly bottom-line-oriented, no-surprises-accepted culture, such as the one induced by Harold Geneen at ITT, warning signals may be ignored, suppressed, or misinterpreted under the pressure of the cultural norm. Organizational culture serves as a shared schema, and information more than mildly contradictory to the schema is ignored (Kiesler and Sproull 1982). A strong analytical culture may develop resistance to ambiguity; a strong performance-oriented culture may develop a resistance to long-term strategic thinking. Indeed, a seriously underemphasized and underresearched aspect of culture is that any strong organizational culture ultimately creates resistance to change: The sails of yesterday become the shackles of tomorrow.

LEVERAGE POINTS FOR EXERCISING STRATEGIC CONTROL

In this and the preceding chapters, we have identified a number of systems and processes that affect an organization's ability to learn from the environment and to adapt to external changes. Such self-regulating adaptation, we have argued, is one of the principal objectives of strategic control. In other words, strategic control is exercised by managing those systems and processes that affect a firm's learning and adaptive capabilities. In this section, we suggest some specific ways in which these controls can be exercised and the possible consequences of such actions.

Managing Perceived Resource Scarcity

Rare are the finance professors who, in their introductory graduate-level courses in corporate finance, do not take a satirical crack at corporations for keeping their internal hurdle rate higher than their adjusted cost of capital. "Look at how many wealth-creating, positive NPV projects you may lose this way," the rhetoric runs, "and yet the best of companies—the IBMs and GEs—practice it." Indeed, from a finance theory point of view, it can never make sense, agency theory notwithstanding. But from a corporate viewpoint, it probably does make sense, since persistent practice by successful organizations is usually a normative guide. An artificial hurdle rate can certainly create undesirable behavioral patterns, but it can also serve as a way of manipulating the internal perception of resource scarcity.

"You cannot get a budget for even whitewashing the toilet in the factory, but the R&D goons can buy just about the fanciest toys and carpets they want." This complaint is not uncommon among many production executives. From time to time, one also comes across companies where the story is reversed. These different treatments are often attributed to corporate values, top managers' origins, the need for image or PR, and a host of other reasons. But such differences also have behavioral consequences, intended or otherwise. Under certain conditions, it may be most efficient to run certain departments in what Kanter (1983) calls the "segmented" way, with clear differentiation of tasks and roles and a tight control on operating efficiency. In other divisions or departments where macroinnovations are required, a lesser degree of resource scarcity may be entirely appropriate.

The experiences of an European and a Japanese consumer electronics company in commercializing new products and models illustrates the effect of such differences in perceived resource scarcity among organizational components. The European company is recognized around the world for its technological innovativeness and has pioneered most of the recent technological breakthroughs in its field. Yet, it has persistently suffered because of its inability to quickly commercialize its own innovations. The Japanese company, in contrast, has historically been a technology follower (though this has now changed) and its key strength has been in enhancing technologies obtained from outside the organization and in fast and efficient introduction of new products in the market.

In both companies, introduction of a new product follows a three-phase process. The basic technology is developed (or acquired and enhanced) in the basic research laboratories. In the next phase, the pre-development laboratories create the product concept and build a working model. Finally, the development laboratories interface with the production system so as to finalize the design for commercial production.

The main difference between the two companies that largely explains the differences in the speed and efficiency with which they can commercialize a new product, lies in the approach and philosophy of the development laboratories. The key task of these laboratories is to debug the design so as to facilitate efficient production. In the Japanese company, when the factory points out a problem, the development group "fixes the problem", i.e., finds the fastest and least cost solution that will overcome the problem without affecting operational performance of the product. In the European company, in contrast, the development laboratory engages in ascertaining the basic reason for the problem and, in the words of one of its managers, "finds the most creative and technically perfect solution to the problem". Often, this leads to significant redesign and though the final product may be technically superior as a result, the actual market introduction of the product is usually delayed quite significantly.

Reasons for these differences in the approach of development laboratories in the two companies lie much more in the management systems and processes of the companies rather than in external variables such as professional norms in the two societies. In the Japanese companies, basic research laboratories are directly and separately funded and are not subjected to rigid operational control or accountability. But, the development laboratories are seen not as constituents of the R&D function but as members of the operating departments. They are not independently funded. Instead they are funded through the development budgets provided to the operating departments. This leads to strict accountability and a much tighter control on resources available to them. In contrast, the development laboratories in the European company are considered as components of the R&D organization and are managed the same way as the basic research and pre-development laboratories. They have, relative to the Japanese company, much greater resources and are subjected to much less accountability. These differences in the internal perception of resource scarcity results in the different approaches and world views of the development laboratories in the two companies. For the European company, the same set of management processes that lead to creativity and innovativeness at the level of basic research also results in delays and inability to make necessary compromises at the level of application and production engineering tasks.

The point is that control on operating and capital budgets may *intentionally* be different in different organizational subunits to match the task demands of these subunits. We know that companies pursue such policies, but we do not often see the function they serve. We have already referred to the OST (Objectives, Strategies, Tactics) system of Texas Instruments. This system may be unique to TI, but the concept is not. Different degrees of resource scarcity in the tactical and strategic processes are common in many successful companies (refer, for instance, to the observation of Peters and Waterman [1982] that in the excellent companies, the skunkworkers always get their supplies). GE executives often mention how easy it is to get resources for "weird ideas," and 3M senior middle managers have little pockets that they can dip into to provide support for some of the unusual, off-the-wall directions that their subordinates wish to pursue.

The overall message is simple. In successful large companies, the internal perception of resource scarcity is managed and controlled. It is differentiated by function, division, and purpose, as illustrated in the consumer electronics example just discussed. That illustration dealt with creating deliberately different perceptions across business functions in order to accomplish a strategically important business purpose. The same phenomena occurs across different business units. In one well-known multinational firm engaged in the industrial products industry, divisions that are not part of the company's strategic thrust are given very high hurdle rates for any new projects. However, as the divisional purpose is to produce high cash flows, investment funds will be made available for, let's say, a new computer application which will give faster inventory turns and quicker receivables collection. Such differentiation serves a strategic purpose and is vital for effective strategic control.

Managing Information Complexity

The key contribution of Lawrence and Lorsch (1967) to organization theory is the insight that the organizational structure must recognize the differences in environmental conditions faced by different subunits and must be designed to cope with such differences. Galbraith (1973) has shown how different kinds of organizational structures have different capabilities of managing information complexity. Combining these insights, one can clearly see how organizational structure can be used as a tool for strategic control.

If the organization faces a complex technological environment with short product lives and new product development as one of its key success factors, one would expect to see overintegration in the R&D and product development functions. This can be achieved through the use of teams and task forces, through use of liaison roles, and an overall undersegmentation or underdifferentiation within the units. During periods of extreme turbulence, the entire organization must show such characteristics to deal with the complexity of the information it must process. In contrast, during periods of relative continuity, or in particular, in departments that need to be insulated, overdifferentiation and careful and well-defined structuring of roles and functions may prevail. We do not elaborate on this issue, since a number of authors have identified the behavioral effects of such differences in organizational structure. We merely point out that differentiating internal structure of the organization so as to create different degrees of information complexity for different subunits may often be a vital element in the overall process of managing change (i.e., in the process of strategic control).

The Internal Information System

The internal management information system serves as a major signal to all members of the organization and is an important force for shaping internal behavior. If the system demands yesterday's facts and figures as inputs for tomorrow's action plans, the message to all managers is one of stability, of continuity. If it demands information about changes not only within the task domain but also beyond it, if it emphasizes that challenges may come from invisible quarters not confronted in the past and demands monitoring for such possibilities, the message of possible discontinuities will be equally clear. If the information system requires only data on deviations from the current quarter's plans, the focus of management attention will be short term. If it seeks information about deviations from long-term expectations of overall demand growth, technology evolution, and competitive responses, the focus will be broader.

Recent research shows that an increasing number of corporations are incorporating information on the sociopolitical, technological, regulatory, and macroeconomic environment in their planning processes (see Klein and Linneman 1984). This is a clear sign of the growing recognition that policy-oriented information as opposed to merely "facts" (Wilensky 1967) is important for setting and changing strategic direction. The rapid progress being made in computer and communications technology and their application to unstructured tasks is expected to revolutionize management information systems, which in turn will have a significant impact on the nature and process of strategic control. This topic, we believe, deserves special attention because of the enormity of its possible impact, and we discuss it separately in greater detail in Chapter 8.

These variables of perceived resource scarcity, information complexity, and internal information systems are in a way overarching influences that affect the entirety of organizational behavior, including the way it manages or copes with change. They drive the enactment process and work as filters or blinders, determining which aspects of the environment are given attention and how those aspects are perceived. With regard to more specific components of the model of organizational adaptation, we suggest that scanning and experimentation are the two key methods for sensitizing the organization to the need for change. In the following paragraphs, we discuss these two instruments for sensitizing and explore the ways they can be used for driving the strategic change process.

Operationalizing Scanning

Scanning is the starting point of the information cycle that drives strategic control. It is the principal source for input of external information, which is then evaluated and analyzed to convert the data into intelligence. This assembled intelligence is then disseminated through the communication process and is used in decision making. This use, in turn, determines further information needs and feeds back into the cycle (see Figure 3.6).

This is the classical concept of scanning, and it assumes that the relevant information can be prespecified and categorized, collected,

*Figure 3.6 The Information Cycle
(Adapted from Montgomery and Weinberg)*

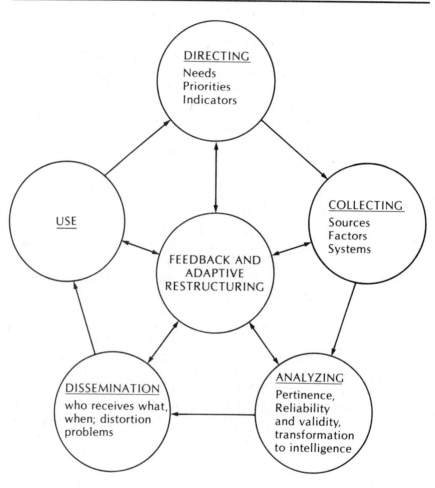

Montgomery and Weinberg, TOWARD STRATEGIC INTELLIGENCE SYSTEMS, Vol. 43 (Fall, 1979). Pg. 44, Fig. 1. Reprinted with permission from American Marketing Association.

analyzed, and passed on to predetermined and nominated users (for an elaboration of this model, see Montgomery and Weinberg 1979). The purpose of the process is to generate information for specific, predetermined use. The model clearly views the world as analyzable, continuous, and predictable.

Under these assumptions, scanning must be focused on strategic thrusts or issues. The critical factors are accuracy and speed. Indeed, in a stable industry, those are the traditional objectives of the scanning system.

But the whole model breaks down under assumptions of discontinuity, unpredictability, and ambiguity. Under those circumstances, determining which information is to be acquired is no longer possible, since threats to strategic thrusts may arise from totally unanticipated sectors. Analyzing the information is also not possible since analysis, in the traditional sense of the term, assumes that the information has one correct meaning and significance, which can be identified if one looks for it hard and close enough. During periods of rapid change, environmental information is often ambiguous and no *one* correct course of action can be drawn analytically. Who might need the information or the uses to which it can be put is also often not clear. In turbulent times, the neat and elegant cycle becomes hopelessly inadequate.

While managing momentum during periods of continuity, scanning must be linked to strategies, just as the strategies must be causally modeled so that the implication of new information can be clearly assessed. When making strategic leaps, at least some aspects of scanning must be deliberately decoupled from current strategies, effectively setting it free to find solutions that can then be applied to problems (Weick 1969). In a stable environment, scanning must be problem triggered; in an unstable environment, it must aim at being information triggered (Collings 1968). Under assumptions of environmental continuity, scanning can use a large amount of investigation and research (i.e., the search mode [Keegan 1967]). In the warlike conditions of unpredictable change, it must depend more on viewing and experimentation. The whole nature and purpose of scanning must be very different under the two scenarios.

Montgomery and Weinberg (1979) have suggested a typology of scanning behavior that is useful in understanding this difference. They categorized the environment using the military classification of extent of relevance (i.e., the immediacy of possible impact). The area of influence (see Figure 3.7) is the immediate task area of the organization—its current task domain. The intermediary area represents areas of activities that are on the periphery of the firm's area of influence (e.g., emerging alternative technologies, suppliers, customers, or competitors), and the area of interest is the broader environment that the company is concerned with and includes relevant social, technological, legal, economic, and political sectors.

Each of the areas influences the short-, medium-, and long-term performance of the firm. In normal times, the influence follows pattern A in the Figure 3.7. Impact on short- and medium-term performance arises only from the area of influence, while long-term performance is also affected by the intermediate zone and the area of interest. During periods of unpredictable and rapid change, how-

Figure 3.7 Scanning Under Strategic Momentum and Strategic Leap Control

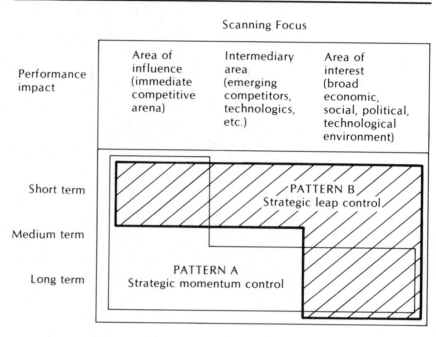

ever, the pattern is entirely different, shown as pattern B in the figure. Short-term performance is affected by developments in all three areas, and medium- and long-term performance are almost entirely determined by changes in the area of interest. Thus, the focus of scanning as well as its specificity must indeed be entirely different, depending on which of the two alternative assumptions the firm makes about its environment (see Ghoshal and Westney, 1984 for a more detailed discussion).

In our earlier discussions on the sensitizing process, we suggested that scanning can have a process effect; that is the nature of induced scanning behavior can affect the assumptions of the firm about its environment as well as the proactiveness with which it is willing to intrude or probe into it. If management induces extensive use of the search mode, both on the part of managers and through the use of external agents or consultants, the organization is gradually going to strengthen its belief that the environment is analyzable (i.e., predictable and continuous) and will also tend to become more analytical. If, instead, experimentation and trial and error are emphasized, the possibility of environmental discontinuities will gradually become more manifest.

Induced scanning behavior can affect the overall strategic orientation of the firm in another way. Feldman and March (1981) have suggested that information serves as signals and symbols within the organization. Manipulating the method of scanning can alter the strength and meaning of this symbolic role of information. When a firm insists on quantitative analysis for any proposal to be accepted, and its CEO obviously appreciates arguments using facts and projections, continuity and linearity in the environment are suggested. In contrast, a firm in which a manager's intuition is accepted as valid logic for proposals, at least as arguments to supplement quantitative analysis, and the CEO is willing to listen to "gut feel," will tend to ultimately generate more intuitive elements. If we perceive the environment to be highly complex, then developing intelligence from information is often not a process of analysis but a process of Gestalt, which can be expressed only as feelings or beliefs and not as logical consequences of past happenings. If Gestalt is to be encouraged, intuition must be accepted. This is another connection that seems to be seldom made, even in highly successful and dynamic corporations.

Promoting Experimentation

When the environment is highly complex, the active organization experiments. It sends out probes and looks at the response. Trial marketing rather than market research becomes more important, as does building prototypes instead of perfecting designs on drawing boards. Experimentation is the key to enactment and a vital mechanism for innovation in an era of discontinuities.

The issue of experimentation is linked to the whole question of organizational entrepreneurship. How can an organization encourage its members to behave entrepreneurially? What structural and process characteristics create the hands-on behavior of excellent companies?

Jarillo (1984) has argued that entrepreneurship must be analytically examined in terms of two dimensions: what makes it desirable (for the entreprenuer) and what makes it feasible. Desirability is seen as a marginal concept; it is the differential desirability between the state if the risks and efforts of entrepreneurship are undertaken versus the state if they are not. In an organizational context, this marginal nature of desirability is crucial, for if the nature of employment provides a totally satisfactory level of attractiveness of a future state if nothing unusual is done, then the marginal benefit of innovation is low and entrepreneurship is impeded. In addition, entrepreneurship in large organizations also involves the question of how to make what is desirable for the company also desirable for the individual or group. Anyone with any experience of large organizations will appreciate that this issue is nontrivial.

Feasibility similarly involves two aspects. Creating the innovation must be feasible for the individual, which usually hinges on the availability of resources, including free time. It must also be feasible for the firm to implement the innovation.

Management of a firm can promote entrepreneurship and experimentation by influencing both desirability and feasibility. Desirability is a composite of the desirability of success (the upside) and the undesirability of failure (the downside). First, the management of a firm can try to increase the size of the upside. The idea sounds simple but presents enormous problems in implementation:

> The traditional modes of reward are, in many cases, ineffective: economic rewards have to be either too small compared with the size of the upside for the organization, or too large for what other members of the organization can accept. Promotions can have the effect of placing people in the wrong places, since being a good, entrepreneurial junior or middle manager is very different from being an effective senior manager, where responsibilities are often of a very different nature. These rewards can indeed be used, but very carefully. (Jarillo 1984).

Decreasing the downside is, however, much easier although less practiced. By rewarding "honest failures," top management can probably foster entrepreneurship more effectively than by any other means. The notion is not new, but it is surprising how few top executives accept the idea of honoring—actually rewarding, not just tolerating—entrepreneurial failures within the firm.

The feasibility issues boils down to the question of resource scarcity discussed earlier. But one of the most crucial and least appreciated resources for entrepreneurship is slack time. Managers, to be entrepreneurial, need a little free time to think, to feel, and to be creative. Further, the need is not just for free time but also for a degree of control over one's time. Thus, another crucial leverage point for promoting innovation within the firm and another key to effective strategic control is to delegate, to the extent possible, control over time to the executives themselves.

A word of caution is appropriate at this stage. We talk about continuity and discontinuity as if one or the other state must be assumed to prevail. This clearly is not true; the environments of most firms have elements of both stability and turbulence. Further, some activities of the firm may face a more stable environment, while others may be subjected to faster change. We recognize that our mode of discussion might suggest polarized thinking; it might not be sufficiently clear that what we have labeled as stability and turbulence are two extremes of a diverse array of environmental states. Absolute stability and absolute instability are abstractions that do not exist in practice. Our objective in delineating these extremes was merely to be more explicit about the differences and not to suggest a dichotomous choice on the part of managers in organizations. In every organization a part of scanning must be domain focused while another must be diverse, probing into the interemediate zone and area of influence. There must be both search and surveillance, both scanning and experimentation. A part of the looking-out process must be highly issues specific, monitoring environmental developments around specific strategic issues and key success factors. Another part must be divorced from currently salient issues, viewing the broad environment for early-early warnings arising beyond the currently understood boundaries of those issues. Herein lies the complexity of managing complex organizations, and we have no intention to suggest otherwise. Our objective in dichotomizing environmental conditions, and hence the nature of strategic change, was to make the whole spectrum analytically clearer by showing the spread between the extremes.

4

Classical Views of Strategic Control: Controlling the Strategic Momentum

In the previous two chapters, we discussed major streams of relevant underlying theoretical dimensions of strategic control to provide the proper basis from which to design a strategic control system that might be useful in meeting the organization's needs. This focused above all on the interrelationships between strategic control and organizational change, the role of relevant environmental analysis and scanning theory (in Chapter 2), and the delineation of what are some critical leverage points for strategic control (in Chapter 3). Recall that Chapter 1 distinguished between controlling the strategic momentum of established strategies and controlling leaps representing new strategic directions. The distinction is based on whether environmental changes can be interpreted as fundamentally reflecting continuity and linearity or discontinuity and major upheavals.

In this chapter, we develop the basics of a strategic control system intended to work in relatively stable conditions when the challenge is to maintain strategic momentum. In particular, we concentrate on the development and measurement of relevant variables. We discuss in detail three broad approaches to such strategic momentum control with their corresponding categories of variable types, namely classical responsibility center control, control based on assessing critical underlying success factors, and control of the basic generic strategies. After discussing each of these three types of strategic momentum control, we elaborate on various mechanisms that may be employed for achieving any of these control types. We conclude the chapter by suggesting an approach to integrating all these measures and approaches into a contingency-based system of strategic momentum control, elaborating on how this system should be tailor-made to different organizational needs.

STRATEGIC MOMENTUM CONTROL

As the starting point for our discussion of the three major approaches to strategic momentum control, let us reiterate the typical context that prevails. An organization would have developed a strategy for competing in a given competitive setting, i.e., within an environment that is characterized by evolution. Even though numerous changes may be going on, they can typically be understood, at least to some extent, as extensions of the present. The environment may thus be seen as changing in a relatively continuous, linear way. Social changes follow a certain evolutionary pattern grounded in the past and in the present. Economic shifts can be seen as stemming from present economic policy. Technological developments are largely based on further incremental extensions of product or process know-how. Changes in the political arena can be understood by examining the political roots of the past and the present. Above all, competitors and customers are identifiable and traceable over time. For all these examples, as well as for many others, a payoff is involved for knowing and understanding the underlying forces that impact and shape the evolution of one's business.

Such peacetime conditions, however, do not imply an Alice in Wonderland setting. Even though some stability is present and the degree of change is manageable, the good old days do not necessarily prevail. On the contrary, changes may be rapid and complex, calling for the utmost in managerial skills, insights, and alertness to cope successfully. However, there is a sense of continuity, of links with the past, and a feeling that one can manage and control this often complex, rapid change pattern.

Strategic momentum control is thus to a significant degree intended to strengthen an organization's ability to deal with a basically linear environment. Above all, it helps the firm to sensitize itself to critical environmental changes so that it can modify and strengthen its strategy in *anticipating* such changes. Responsibility center control, one form of strategic momentum control, is based primarily on measuring actual performance deviation against a standard. Other strategic momentum control approaches are more heavily based on articulating underlying environmental assumptions, monitoring changes in these, and examining whether a change in one's strategy should take place when such environmental shifts are identified.

In at least three ways the strategic momentum control processes can help management understand and deal with the potential impact of environmental changes on their strategy. First, *time* is of the essence. Early realization of changes in critical environmental factors might lead to corrective action at a time when the span of options might still be relatively wide. Late awareness and acknowledgment of key environmental shifts, on the other hand, are often a handicap, because fewer choices for correction are available.

Second, the very attempt to be sensitive to a particular factor can increase management's ability to understand and predict it. Such sensitivity should result in more clearly focused internal, analytical, and data-based research efforts to increase the organization's understanding of a particular phenomenon.

Third, through active efforts, a firm can increase its own response potential to environmental changes. One way to accomplish this is by investing in more flexibility. This could be manifested by the choice of equipment—for example, by building an industrial power generator in such a way that it can alternatively burn gas, oil, or coal—or by investing in a broader product line, thereby allowing a more flexible response to different competitive pressures (Lorange 1980). Thus, situations exist in which added cost might legitimately be incurred to increase a firm's flexibility in responding to critical environmental factors to maintain the risk of a strategy at an acceptable level. Choosing the cheapest alternative can be expensive in the long run. An excessive concentration on buying flexibility must also be guarded against, on the other hand, to avoid wasting of resources.

RESPONSIBILITY CENTER CONTROL

Clearly, peacetime strategic control cannot be based solely on monitoring shifts in environmental assumptions and reassessing their potential impacts on objectives and strategic programs. Measures of performance based on actual versus intended outputs are also necessary. Taken *together* with critical environmental assumption measures, such measures of market share, profits, costs, and so on constitute the measurement package of the peacetime strategic control system.

In most typical management control systems, the fundamental unit of analysis is a responsibility center. This is an identifiable unit of an organization under the supervision of one person who has considerable discretion for impacting performance. The responsibilities of such individuals will vary depending on which decisions are within their control and which are handled elsewhere. The five commonly used forms of responsibility centers are cost centers, revenue centers, profit centers, investment centers, and discretionary expense centers. A recent survey by Reece and Cool (1978) demonstrates uses of the various types of responsibility centers and the prominence of ROI-based investment centers in particular. Vancil (1973) has discussed when which type of responsibility center is most appropriate, depending on the strategic role the responsibility center is intended to play. No particular type of responsibility center is "best" in all circumstances; the type of responsibility control that is most appropriate depends on the particular strategic tasks intended for the given case. We review these various responsibility center uses next.

Cost Centers

Cost centers are responsibility centers in which the manager is held responsible only for controlling cost inputs (see Figure 4.1). In a manufacturing department, these would be costs of direct labor and raw materials, as well as the assigned share of common costs—for heat, central staff activities, the computer, and so on—that the organization believes it should be charging. Typically, all of this is codified in the familiar form of an expense budget. However, additional considerations may call for other measures such as a careful head count of personnel; the cost center manager may be held accountable for variables that cannot be tracked solely in dollar terms.

In the normal expense budget, two important distinctions ought to be made. The first is to distinguish *for each* responsibility center those elements that are largely controllable by the manager involved. Some items may be noncontrollable, and therefore the manager does not have decision authority. To include such items in a management control report, mixed in with the controllable, is to make a mockery of the system. Such noncontrollable items should be dealt with separately.

The next important distinction is between three different classes of costs on the input side, namely engineered, discretionary (some-

Figure 4.1   Cost Center Control

times called managed), and fixed costs. Engineered costs are any costs that are based on an explicit, specified physical relationship with a selected measure of activity. Discretionary costs are costs that arise from periodic (usually yearly) appropriation decisions that directly reflect top management policies regarding the maximum permissible amounts to be incurred, and that do not have a demonstrable optimum relationship between inputs (as measured by the costs) and outputs (as measured by sales service or production) (Horngren 1972, 242). The important point here is that discretionary costs should be controlled in a different way from engineered costs.

Despite no direct reference to this appearing in the control report, control is exercised by means of two important nuances. If discretionary costs did not exist, no trigger would be available to check the expenditure. Variance in this case therefore causes the question to be raised: Is the new program worthwhile? The second way in which control is exercised is through the negotiation and establishment of the budget in the first place. This provides the occasion for the cost item itself to be examined. For example, should we use the central computer or buy our own mini-computers? Only after having established the basic policy can the budgeting allocations be negotiated. The budget, with discretionary costs, serves as a commitment as to what is acceptable from management's point of view. It does not signify the *correct* amount. Control has to be exercised with this in mind.

Discretionary costs are largely driven by the strategic intention of the organization, assuming a high degree of rationality by the organization. They are costs incurred today to build up a certain strategic position for the future. As such, we can say that the discretionary costs are representative of the strategic budget of the corporation. A close focus on the use of discretionary funds is therefore critical to ensure realistic strategy implementation. Without separating out the discretionary costs, one could easily succumb to the temptation to "borrow" from this discretionary resource pool to bail oneself out when faced with difficulties in meeting engineered cost targets due to operating problems. Texas Instruments pioneered an approach to this by developing a separate categorization for strategic expenditures to carry out the strategic activities of the company, clearly separating it from the operating activities and operating budget. Thus, the profits shown in its operating budget would have to be adjusted for budgeted strategic expenses to reach budgeted organization profits (Lorange and Vancil 1977).

Fixed or committed costs are the third input category. These are costs such as depreciation on machinery, which have been committed in some prior period and which cannot now be changed. In these cases, the basic decision has already been made, and typically, it cannot be reversed. The expense center manager may have control of how much of the resource in question (for example, a specific machine tool) is used. If a standard charge per hour is employed, and the expense center manager's usage goes up, the manager might show a negative variance. Strategic considerations should dictate what activity levels should be chosen (i.e., that market conditions should dominate such judgments). Cost allocation items stemming from past decisions should not dominate such strategic decisions. Often, however, critical responses to the environment are hampered by cost utilization considerations. Using such committed numbers as part of the ongoing control process may thus raise problems.

Note, however, that control over committed costs is normally exercised at the time the resource commitment is made—for instance, at the time of purchase of a particular asset. This may be part of a separate control system: the capital budget. It is critical that the capital budget be explicitly derived from the particular strategies in question. Often, hurdle rate considerations play such a dominant role that the testing of the underlying rational for the strategy merits checking. How does the investment hold up in relation to critical success factors that are not properly addressed? The key check is the overall viability of the strategy, of which the particular assets invested are only one part. In any event, the engineered, discretionary, and committed expense items all require different methods of planning and control. This is an important reason for carefully separating them.

To summarize, cost centers are the simplest form of responsibility centers. Broadly speaking, they refer to keeping track of any relevant inputs to the responsibility center, although in practice their role is normally restricted to dollars. These dollars need to be separated into different classifications if control is to be effective. First necessity is distinguishing between controllable and noncontrollable items, and second between engineered, discretionary, and committed costs. Maintaining these basic distinctions is necessary if control using expense centers is to be effective. Appropriate cost center control requires an understanding of the philosophical viewpoint of a strategic budget. Such costs are associated with building a strategic position in the future by using present resources for strategic purposes. In an operating budget, on the other hand, one accounts for those costs having to do with ongoing, business-as-usual activities. Unfortunately, cost center control often confuses strategic and operating costs, thereby making it much more difficult to exercise proper peacetime strategic control. Because of the seeming simplicity of cost center control, this dimension of the control often receives insufficient attention.

Revenue Centers and Profit Centers

The second basic type of responsibility center is the revenue center. In such a center, one measures the manager solely by output (i.e., the revenues brought in). For the purpose of this discussion, we consider the revenue center as part of the next type of responsibility center, the so-called profit center. In such a system, one measures the manager by both input and output (i.e., revenue less expenses yields the profit picture) (see Figure 4.2).

The reason for such a responsibility center stems from a potential fundamental weakness with cost center or revenue center control. If a cost center or a revenue center manager is being pushed hard to meet expenses (input goals) or revenue targets (output goals), the manager always has the option to slacken off on the dimension that is not being measured, either the output or the input dimension. Producing less or incurring more costs, which are not measured, makes it easier for the manager to meet input goals or output goals respectively, which are being measured. With profit centers, the direct measurement of inputs *and* output removes this potential weakness, although it raises some issues of its own. Each of three basic organizational situational settings raises different concerns with respect to how to measure revenue and thereby profits pragmatically.

Setting One: Open Market. When the profit center boundaries are the same as the legal boundaries of the organization, the simplest possible revenue measurement situation exists. Since the product is being sold in the open market, the revenue results from the market price of the product (or service) sold. No complications are involved. The profit center manager seeks to maximize profits by finding the right price-volume relationship consistent with low expenses.

If instead of one such profit center the organization has a series of these, each of which sells only to the outside and not to each other, and each market is largely independent of the others, then the measurement problem is equally simple. Freestanding operating divisions within a divisionalized firm are, for instance, usually considered as separate profit centers; typically, virtually no interaction exists between them, and they all sell in different markets.

Figure 4.2 Profit Center Control

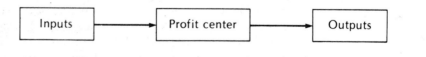

One potential problem is worth noting. There may be a joint service department, such as a central computer group, whose costs have to be allocated between two divisions. This affects the expense picture and it may be a difficult issue to come up with a fair formula for allocating such joint costs. Thus, this picture of independent profit centers rarely holds across all of a corporation unless virtually everything is decentralized; having a clear separation of all revenues and costs is unusual.

Setting Two: Imperfect Market.   More often, profit centers interact with each other, and intermediate markets are frequently imperfect. Suppose, for example, that at Ford Motor Company, profit center 1 is a foundry making engine blocks, and that profit center 2 and profit center 3 are the assembly divisions for Ford and Lincoln Mercury, respectively. The Ford division, let us say, buys all its engine blocks from the block division. The market is imperfect, because buying the same engine block from other foundries is not possible. If the block division is to be a profit center, then it must charge a price to the other divisions. Since no good open market exists (no other company's engine block is exactly the same), the price must be arrived at through some system. In this case, it would usually be based on the cost of making the block. Since cost issues play an important role in such price negotiations, the role of cost in the workings of responsibility centers is central. However, since so many assumptions are involved in arriving at the cost of a block, the final number will be to some extent arbitrary.

Thus, bargaining is an essential ingredient when an imperfect intermediary market exists. The potential problem is that relative bargaining power rather than strategic considerations might determine which activity levels are being pursued. The important dimension, from a strategic point of view, is the overall competitiveness of the final products in relation to those turned out by competitors. The competition has no interest in internal cost transfers within the corporation. A realistic total cost picture must be generated, and strategic decisions must be taken on the basis of this assessment, not on the basis of fragmented cost pictures arising from limited views of profit centers operating in a near-term adversary bargaining setting.

With an imperfect intermediary market, profit center 2—the Ford assembly division in our example—may not have the option of going to an alternate supplier for the blocks. Design secrets or quality control may have led top management to forbid such a move. Time delays and the risk of supply interruptions may make the alternative unattractive to profit center 2 management. Under such conditions, the bargaining strength of profit center 1 is much enhanced. They have a captive customer. The operation of profit centers under such conditions creates the risk that the broader strategic picture can become distorted.

Setting Three: Mixed Market. The third basic type of setting within which profit centers operate is one in which a reasonably open market exists for each product, and where the divisions can, in theory, choose whether to sell to each other or whether to the open market. Similarly, they can buy internally or externally. This setting can occur with two types of products. The first type is the proprietary product—for example, the nameplate on a washing machine, which requires no special technology to make, uses general-purpose equipment, and has a low setup cost. The second type is the general-purpose product that is widely available—for example, bolts, switches, and so forth. In these cases, an active open market exists in which prices already are available or can easily be established. Under such conditions, the buying division gets bids from inside and outside the company, and makes purchasing decisions on the basis of price and its estimate of other factors such as quality and delivery.

Such a system can work effectively if the following two conditions hold:

1. Profit center managers are each free to buy or sell as they see fit. No captive markets exist, with the result that genuine arm's-length bargaining occurs.
2. Good access to information among divisions exists (i.e., each division understands the markets, prices, and costs that the others are facing).

These two rules do not always hold—in which case modifications to the system have to be made. The basic difficulty under this situation is the danger that by maximizing the division's profit, the manager may not be maximizing the organization's profit. This occurs, for example, when idle capacity is in division 2, but division 1, because it receives a better price, buys outside.

Profit centers can, in summary, be discussed as one of three basic types of responsibility centers, wherein the manager is held accountable for inputs (expenses) and outputs (revenues). Broadly speaking, profit centers might be better referred to as output centers. Dollar profit is almost exclusively used in practice, but a responsibility center's output often includes other aspects: quality, delivery performance, ongoing maintenance levels, increase in market share, and increase in sales. Particularly in the case of poor markets, the measuring of profit may be so difficult and arbitrary as to be counterproductive. Establishing goals and rewarding performance along the dimensions of other output measures could be far more successful.

An ultimate concern of top management is likely to be the maintenance of a basis for long-run profit. However, the key variables that influence future strategic positions may have little to do with short-term reported profit. As has been documented by many, a profit center emphasis taken out of strategic context certainly might hamper strategic progress in the long run when short-term viewpoints become too dominant.

INVESTMENT CENTERS

Investment centers form the fourth basic type of responsibility center (see Figure 4.3). An investment center adds a concern for the amount of assets employed to generate a particular economic result. To produce a $5 million profit using capital assets of $1 million is a much more spectacular performance than to do the same with capital assets of $100 million. All organizations are likely to be concerned at one stage or another with the effectiveness with which they are using their assets. Typically, this concern is with physical assets, such as plant and equipment, inventory, raw materials, and the like. More recently, some concern has also arisen about the utilization of other organizational assets, such as human resources, a topic to which we return later.

Investment centers are the dominant form of responsibility centers in decentralized organizations (Anthony and Dearden 1980, 277). The most common measure used in such cases is return on investment (ROI), a term familiar to most people in organizations. Residual income is perhaps the next most popular measure and defined as income after the deduction of assets employed, multiplied by a percentage that represents the minimum percentage return expected on the company's capital. Before looking at these measures

Figure 4.3   Investment Center Control

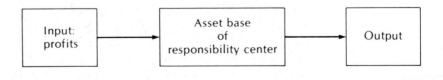

in detail, reviewing the basic components of ROI is useful. As noted, this measure has widespread use. A survey by Reece and Cool (1978) of Fortune 1,000 firms found that the percentage of respondents using ROI to evaluate performance of their investments increased from 52 percent to 65 percent between 1966 and 1976. The proportion of respondents using ROI with an alternative measure, residual income, declined substantially from 41 percent to 28 percent during the same period. The proportion of those using residual income alone declined from 6 percent to 2 percent. These survey responses led Reece and Cool to conclude that "despite the pitfalls of . . . using ROI . . . most companies . . . seem to feel that the best approach is to use ROI" (1978, 28).

The asset base is normally divided into two parts: fixed and so-called current assets. Fixed assets primarily include land, buildings, and equipment, while current assets consist of cash, accounts receivable, inventory, and any other items of working capital.

Two major problems are associated with measuring the asset base. The first is the question of what to include, and each organization has its own answer. Some include all assets; some exclude certain classes. The criteria for inclusion ought to be based first on purpose. If the ROI is to be used for economic evaluation of new projects, different elements would be included than would be if the measure was to be used for management control purposes. The items relevant for management control are only those under the responsibility center manager's control. For example, cash and marketable securities are elements of the asset base, but many companies with central cash management give the treasurer absolute jurisdiction over these assets to minimize the organization's float. When the treasurer has such control, holding the investment center manager responsible may be unreasonable and this item would be excluded from the base.

This question, which appears simple in this example, rapidly gets more difficult. For example, if managers are not allowed to sell their buildings and make a move, should they be charged with the buildings in their asset base? As a practical matter, all such questions should be answered by asking which items are under each manager's control. If the manager can influence the disposition of the building in a significant way, then including it in the base is reasonable. If the asset bases of two managers differed only on the matter of inclusion or exclusion of their buildings, their ROIs would still look different. Clearly, if one division manager were compared with the other on the basis of such ROI numbers, the result would be misleading, whereas comparing each manager to his own plan, using these measures, would be reasonable.

The second major problem with the asset base is the question of how to measure fixed assets. There are four obvious methods, but only two are widely used, namely gross book value (GBV) and net book value (NBV). Replacement cost and economic value, although conceptually desirable, are rarely used. More recently, the suggestion has been made that the numbers of both of the historical cost methods GBV and NBV be modified by a general price index to allow for inflation. However, even when this is done, it does not significantly alter the nature of the underlying base.

The primary argument for utilizing GBV or NBV is that of objectivity and consistency with the financial statements. The problems associated with all-pervasive linkage to financial accounting in management control systems have been noted previously. The major limitation for management control imposed by using the financial accounting base as its measurement tool is that any return number using historical cost will bear no necessary relationship to normal economic return. Such ROI numbers are arbitrary and have no necessary economic significance. They can be misleading, a potentially serious issue when people in the organization may believe that it reflects an actual economic return. Even though the ROI number is often nonsense from an economic standpoint, it does not mean that it cannot be used for planning and management control purposes. For this purpose, it is an index number, and the comparison over time and against plan is what is important. However, even for these purposes, the accounting base has some limitations. We look at each in turn.

Net Book Value. In calculating ROI, by far the greatest number of organizations use net book value (NBV). Its advantages as presented in the literature seem to be two. The dominant one is its match with the accounting statements—the asset values are the same. It has the further (illusory) advantage of automatically showing the declining value of assets over time through the deduction of depreciation. The difficulty here is that there is no reason to believe that in reality depreciation will match economic wear and tear.

Offsetting these advantages from a management control point of view is that when using NBV, the manager's ROI may increase even if performance is identical to that of the previous year. With an automatically declining asset base (assuming no additions) due to depreciation, such a situation can occur. This effect is often small and would not be of overriding concern in itself, but it is most important when comparing an investment center to some standard, either an industry norm or another division in the same company. If the investment center being evaluated has an asset life and age distribution significantly different from the standard, then misleading figures are generated.

Gross Book Value. The second most popular means of measuring asset value is gross book value (GBV). Again, there is a match to accounting values. Du Pont, who was a pioneer in the use of ROI, apparently chose to use GBV for reasons that in retrospect seem arbitrary (Jerome 1961). However, with this lead from a well-managed innovative company, many other organizations followed suit without questioning Du Pont's logic.

GBV has considerable less attraction for usage after the first few years. The reduction in value of the assets is not reflected (although it does avoid the automatic ROI increases due to depreciation). With the passage of time, the original cost numbers represent little more than an index, with minimal direct economic or managerial content.

A variation on GBV has been suggested recently. With inflation running at unprecedented rates in many countries, financial statements are undergoing even more obvious distortion. Concern has reached the point where some companies are adjusting GBV by a general price index to account for inflation (Klaassen 1976). From a control standpoint, it has some advantages in that it maintains asset values at a level more consistent with the profit calculations. If profit is largely in 1986 dollars, and the asset base is in 1976 dollars, the resulting ratio can be most peculiar.

In summary, GBV and NBV suffer from slightly different disadvantges, but overriding all the arguments for both of them is their direct connection with the financial accounting system. To many, this is seen as an advantage. Although such a measure serves a useful purpose, it must be recognized that it is the result of applying a set of accounting rules that have *no* necessary connection with the economic facts. The difficulty is the widespread assumption by managers that it does have some economic meaning. This basic misconception may make it difficult to interpret investment center performance as part of a broader set of strategic control measures. For this reason, we prefer the next alternative.

Current Market Value. The third method of asset valuation used for ROI is that of current market value. This represents the cash value of the assets, or put another way, the opportunity cost reflected in the resources tied up in the assets. This view of the assets gives an ROI measure that reflects in a crude way the return the manager is deriving from the value of the assets the organization is effectively employing. If the organization were to choose to eliminate a line of business and shift the resources elsewhere, this measure of ROI is an indication of the current return.

From a management control standpoint, such a measure does not significantly aid in the comparison between managers. Those with old facilities and a low market value will have a higher ROI than those with new facilities. However, the control system does provide signals with reference to which divisions are employing the organization's investable resources in the most effective way. To this extent, low ROI numbers provide management with an indication of where to focus their attention. Thus, this measure is particularly helpful when management is pursuing a value-creating approach for its stockholders (Marakon Assoicates 1980; Rappaport 1981; Strategic Planning Assoicates, Inc. 1984).

The prinicpal disadvantages of this method is that it is often hard to get sufficiently objective market values. Although the value of many assets can be determined because a second-hand market exists, or accurate appraisal is possible, for many others this is not the case. This difficulty primarily prevents its use.

Replacement Value. The replacement value form of measurement also has much attraction. The replacement cost of most assets is usually possible to determine. Replacement cost is regularly estimated for fire insurance purposes, and these or similar numbers can be made use of. If the objective of the valuation is to be useful for management control (as opposed to objectivity for financial accounting), obtaining such numbers may well be worth the extra effort.

The value of this measurement for management control lies in the closeness of the asset base assessment to its actual economic value. The return (subject to profit being measured reasonably) is a number that can be used to compare different strategies and their business managers, since each has its asset base measured on a comparable basis of value. This has obvious implications for the determination of management incentives. Some difficulties are also associated with this measure, however. In addition to the measurement problem, a more serious challenge is the potential shift in asset values through events not controlled by the manager. For example, a sharp rise in land values may be a particular area of concern. This difficulty can be dealt with in part by ensuring that the ROI number is not used in isolation but put in context with other measures in the strategic control system.

Depreciation. Another difficulty in adequately measuring responsibility center control imposed by accounting convention is the effect of the measurement of depreciation on the asset base and on profit. The depreciation rules coupled with the type of asset value used in calculations can markedly affect the ROI reported (Dearden 1960).

The key question from a strategic control point of view is to ask what the depreciation policy will motivate managers to do. In all cases, but especially when using composite depreciation and NBV, the control system has the unfortunate side effect of tending to motivate managers to make incorrect investment decisions. Again, focusing on investment decision in a proper strategic context is necessary. By focusing only on the depreciable asset dimension of a strategic commitment, one easily ends up with distorted decisions.

A general conclusion regarding responsibility center performance measurements is that a similar dilemma exists with regard to the measurements of all such types of centers. On the one hand, we may choose to make use of relatively standard accounting-based measures, resulting in indexes of performance for each particualr responsibility center. These indexes present a reasonable picture of how performance is evolving over time but draw an inadequate picture of cross-responsibility center performance differences and provide little insight regarding the strategic significance of particular performance measurement variations. On the other hand, we can adopt more tailor-made economic-based measurements, which unfortunately tend to be much more difficult to determine, primarily because of lack of sufficiently reliable market-based information. The subjectivity of such measurements do not necessarily present a major problem in connection with their use in a strategic control context. The added relevance of such performance data makes them much more readily reconcilable with the other types of measurements that go into a strategic control system. Above all, this type of assessment allows more accurate comparison of the strategic performance of one business relative to the strategic performance of other businesses. As discussed in the next section, the ability to compare strategic performance across businesses is particularly important for divisionalized companies that operate in many businesses. With vertically integrated companies, the comparison across businesses tends to be relatively less important. In these companies, comparison over time is probably relatively more critical.

The purpose of our review of the major responsibility center measurement problems has been twofold: to highlight and make more explicit the many key assumptions underlying the various measurement approaches, and to point out alternative measurement approaches that can provide a more adequate picture of economic values and thus make these measures more readily reconcilable with relevant strategic issues. Given that responsibility center measurements of an organization's performance are an integral part of a strategic momentum control approach, being explicit about these measurement issues is particularly critical, so as to allow for a more realistic reconciliation with other control measures and provide the basis for a common interpretation of strategic performance from this multidimensional set of measures.

Responsibility centers play an important role in practical life.

Maybe the most fundamental potential problem with the use of responsibility center–based performance measures stems from a common lack of reconciliation with the strategic context within which the businesses find themselves, often due to the budgeting process not being properly linked to the planning process but rather being largely a function of the historical budgetary pattern that has been followed in the past. In such circumstances, the planning activity is not adequately coupled to the budgetary process and the accompanying responsibility center control. Planning then becomes important only during certain periods of the year. For the rest of the year, a more narrow, decoupled responsibility center control comes in focus. A lack of understanding of what the measures mean in a strategic context will thus easily occur. In the next section, we discuss how to link responsibility center control with control of the basic underlying critical success factors driving the strategy.

CLASSICAL STRATEGIC PLANNING AS A MODE OF STRATEGIC CONTROL

Most corporations go through the process of developing a set of strategic plans on an annual basis. This typically consists of the development of a set of objectives for the corporation as a whole as well as for each of its businesses. This step is then followed by the development of a set of strategic programs to articulate how to achieve the objectives, emphasizing which organizational entities within the corporation should be involved in what dimensions of the various aspects of objectives implementation. These strategic plans typically culminate in a set of actions that are reflected in the annual budget and which represent the next year's effort toward implementing the objectives and strategic programs. This strategic planning process is typically interactive and iterative. Many corporations have had extensive experience with such processes, and the general recognition seems to be that this is a useful management tool.

From a strategic control point of view, the annual strategic planning process offers an opportunity for the corporation to reexamine its basic strategic direction as well as the validity of the strategic implementation programs being pursued. Thus, one might say that the annual strategic planning process offers a periodical comprehensive review of the robustness of the strategic direction and the relevance of the implementation efforts. The basic direction of the strategy and its implementational effort is thereby controlled.

For many corporations, the annual strategic planning process represents the only basic strategic control effort undertaken. Critical directional and implementational issues are addressed once per year, and at that point, a realignment of the key strategic issues may take place. Properly done, this approach can yield considerable value; however, it also presents several potential problems and shortcomings. An obvious one is the typical tardiness of this strategic control. Most plans, once written, tend to become obsolete relatively quickly, but these out-of-date plans will normally still prevail until the next year's planning effort. Thus, this strategic control tends to be sluggish. Even more important, since in executives' minds the planning activity takes place only once per year—when the calendar indicates that it is time to submit new updated strategic plans—strategic planning and control issues are often forgotten in the periods of the year when planning is not mandated by schedule.

Another problem with this strategic control approach is that many strategic planning processes have tended to become overly bureaucratic, mechanistic, unrealistic, and out-of-touch with critical issues. They take the form of incremental, extrapolative, overly formalistic exercises with heavy grounding in the past, rather than serving as vehicles for taking a zero-based view of what strategies are needed, given the environmental and competitive realities at a given point in time. In such planning approaches, little strategic control benefit accrues.

Note, however, that many corporations follow annual strategic planning approaches that do include effective control and that avoid the pitfalls just indicated. For such corporations, strategic planning can be a useful part of the peacetime strategic control approach.

Forward-Forward and Forward Control of Critical Underlying Success Factors

Monitoring the environmental assumptions that underlie a particular *objective* is important. By systematically assessing such environmental assumptions, management may receive critical early warning signals regarding the continued validity of the objective in its present form. If important environmental factors change substantially, the organization presumably would want to reexamine whether the objective itself is still relevant or whether modification is required. Such a reassessment might detect signals *before* changes in the measurement of the objective itself as exemplified by shifts in, say, market share or financial performance make it evident that the strategic direction should be changed.

Environmental changes may also impact the continued validity of the present form of the implementation efforts to achieve a particular objective—the various strategic programs that are being pursued. Hence, a key issue in assessing the continued viability of a *strategic program* is to reexamine the degree to which the basic underlying environmental assumptions behind the program are still valid. For instance, have the firm's principal competitors reacted as expected? If a stronger-than-expected competitor countermove resulted, does the organization need to modify any of its own competitive moves, such as pricing, advertising, service efforts, and so forth? Changes in technology can also be crtical. Has the firm, for instance, reassessed its basic approach to R&D for this particular strategic program in light of pertinent new research or developments that have surfaced while the strategic program implementation effort was being carried out? Such a reassessment may prompt an organization to reconsider a program's feasibility and may trigger a major reorientation of the strategic program. A third example relates to assumptions about what reactions to expect from various public sector authorities and other external stakeholder groups. For a chemical company, for instance, changing regulations and public attitudes toward hazardous waste may be critical to the continued viability of certain types of strategic programs.

These examples illustrate the importance of monitoring the validity of the basic rationale behind a strategic program to see whether a need for modification exists. The implementation of strategic programs must be understood in a dynamic context in which the organization's own moves can induce responses from outside forces, such as competitors or customers. Implementation moves may thus often necessitate a subsequent modification, redefinition, or redirection of a strategic program; hence, environmental assumption analysis is critical for reassessing a strategic program's continued effectiveness. More traditional project management control measures typically do not adequately highlight environmental factors. Strategic momentum control should make it potentially easier for management to cultivate a dynamic, adaptive, and flexible viewpoint toward upgrading strategic programs over time.

The previous discussion shows the need to strengthen control beyond classic financial responsibility center monitoring. Peacetime strategic control should thus include an emphasis on monitoring changes in *competitive position,* most notably by controlling for changes in a firm's relative market share. An even more forward-looking step to detect early signs of trouble is attention to changes in *critical underlying environmental assumptions,* such as competitors' moves (in R&D, new capacity investments, new product introductions, and so on), consumer behavior, changes in distribution channels, and so forth. Assumptions regarding cost advantages rela-

Figure 4.4 Making Strategic Momentum Control More Anticipatory

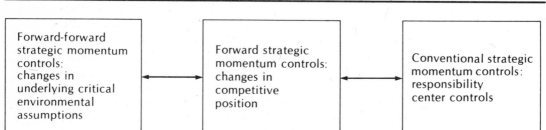

tive to the competition are also relevant. Changes in relative market share might, for instance, indicate shifts in relative cost advantages. Figure 4.4 illustrates how one can strengthen peacetime strategic control. Moving from right of the figure toward the left in an additive manner allows for an earlier warning that modifications in strategic direction or strategic implementation (or both) may be needed.

Management will have to impose practical limits on the list of critical assumptions that can be followed. Typically, a few factors are particularly critical for a given business. Focusing on the most appropriate set of factors requires skill, experience, and intuition in addition to state-of-the-art analytical abilities. (Rockart 1979) Positive as well as negative potential effects from these factors should be kept in mind when determining their importance. Management often tends to be exlusively concerned with threatening factors. Environmental shifts that create opportunities are also critical. Managers must exercise careful judgment when deciding what is truly important to a business and what is not. As discussed later in this chapter, different organizational archetypes need to emphasize different factors in their delineation of key variables.

Once the key factors that affect a particular strategy have been isolated, management should develop a more explicit understanding of how each might evolve. Here, management should operate as social scientists. An eclectic, multidisciplinary approach is typically called for. Managers can draw on theories, conceptual schemes, and analytical techniques from a broad variety of disciplines. The analysis may be based on internal or external sources. It might include making use of econometric data bases (such as Data Resources, Inc., Wharton Econometrics, or Chase Econometrics), financial performance data bases (such as Compustat or Value-Line), business-line competitive position-performance data bases (such as PIMS), or a combination of these or other data bases. Many relevant underlying disciplines can be tapped for developing insight into critical assumptions, including marketing research, demographic and socio-economic analysis, technological forecasting, and industrial economics. Expert panels and delphi-techniques may be used as well. The overriding aim is to develop as comprehensive an understanding as possible of how a key factor might evolve, based on whatever combination of relevant information and know-how is available. Drawing on a multitude of sources—internal as well as external—is important in the course of such probing, managers must develop a sense for whether a particular prediction about the environment is likely to hold true.

In Chapter 5 we review several approaches to such in-depth analysis aimed at developing deeper insights about key phenomena. The fundamental first step, however, is to develop a robust set of key variables. We now turn to a more systematic discussion of this task.

Identification of Key Variables

Having demonstrated the need for a forward-oriented emphasis to peacetime strategic control so that it may play a de facto role as an early warning or an early opportunity–spotting system, we now focus on how to specifically operationalize such an approach. The starting point is the identification of key variables. Recall that key variables are those judged to have major impact (potential or actual) on one's strategic success. They may be directly related to a particular strategic direction or to specific strategic programs intended for implementing a particular strategic thrust. The question in all cases is: Which factors are the critical ones in connection with the particular objectives and strategic programs of the organization? We build on the early work of Rockart (1979) in our approach to these issues, notably the concept of *critical success factors*.

Let us approach this question by examining how one might delineate key variables for a particular business element, positioned in a given product-market segment, with reference both to objectives and to strategic programs. We delineate two classes of factors that should typically be addressed with regard to assumptions behind business-level objectives: factors that affect business attractiveness and those that can lead to changes in the general competitive climate within the particular business niche in question.

The first class of factors, *business attractiveness*, is closely related to the expected future growth pattern of the particular business niche. A rich body of marketing research literature is devoted to the identification of factors that influence the future life cycle of a product in a given market niche (Abell and Hammond 1979). We do not repeat this discussion here, but four sets of pertinent questions seem to emerge from this literature: First, How strong is the growth rate expected to be? Second, What absolute levels of business volume will this niche represent a few years hence? Third, In the case of an emerging business, *when* is the likely takeoff point for a more accelerated growth (i.e., will the timing be soon or possibly much later in an uncertain future)? Finally, What factors might dampen the growth expectation, causing the business to level out or decline? The underlying factors behind these four questions should all be indentified and monitored.

The second class of factors, the general *business climate*, refers to the overall industrial structure within which the business niche is situated. The number of competitors may change, development toward general overcapacity might occur in the niche, or discipline might be lacking in the competitive approach of the particular business, as exemplified by increased price cutting, and so on. It is important to monitor whether the general business climate is improving or worsening and to identify environmental factors that can be used for such assessments. Again, we do not review the well-documented body of knowledge that pertains to this issue but refer the reader to the standard industry analysis literature (Caves 1964; Porter 1980).

Let us now move to the strategic control of the implementation effort for a particular product-market-based business element strategy. We thus have to focus on factors that might impact on the success of particular strategic programs. At least four different types of environmental factors need to be monitored to follow the implementation effort. First, there is the question of the response of the competition to meet the challenges posed by the organization's strategic programs. The competition will not likely let another firm roll out strategic programs without generating responses. Whatever reliable indications can be identified regarding competitor reactions should be monitored. A second factor to be monitored is whether customers are responding to the new product or service (or both) in the intended way. Third, in some businesses, particularly in high-tech fields such as for instance electronics or bioengineering, new strategic programs are particularly sensitive to certain assumptions regarding the technological considerations for making or breaking the particular strategic program. It is necessary to constantly monitor whether such tehnological considerations seem to be holding. Finally, there might be broader environmental stakeholder reactions to a particular strategic program, from interest groups such as the government, consumer advocates, the firm's stockholders, and so on. Reactions of these groups should be monitored in assessing the success of a particular strategic program and in determining whether ameliorating corrective actions are necessary.

The prior discussion can be illustrated by an example taken from the brewery industry (adapted from Lorange 1984). Consider a corporation that started out as a small brewery making pilsner beer but which, as it grew, first diversified horizontally into making other beers and then expanded into related businesses, such as soft-drink bottling and manufacturing of packaging items: glass bottles, closures, and carton containers for its own as well as for outside customers. As can be seen in Figure 4.5, the formal organizational structure reflects considerable vertical integration, and much of what is produced in one division tends to be for a sister division customer. This organizational structure enabled the cost-efficient operation of a large-volume, small-margin, essentially mature business. It reflected a high degree of specializtion, avoidance of duplication, and utilization of scale economies—all essential requirements for success in these types of businesses. An elaborate but conventional responsibility center control system was in place.

With increased competition as well as with changes in customer tastes and purchasing behavior trends, however, the corporation believed it necessary to delineate a strategic control approach for the specific businesses within which it was competing and to monitor progress relative to specific strategic plans for each of these businesses. The strategic structure on which plans and strategic control were based was developed according to the businesses within which the firm was active (see Figure 4.6).

Note that the company chose to see its strategic position in terms of two business levels. The *business elements* are well-delineated product-market entities, for which a relatively unambiguous assessment of the business's future attractiveness can be made and

Figure 4.5   A Formal (Operating) Organizational Structure

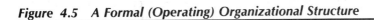

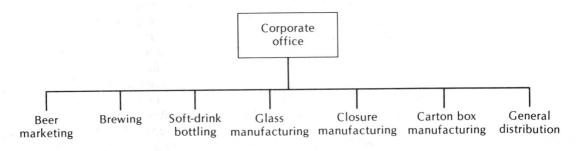

Figure 4.6   A Strategic Structure

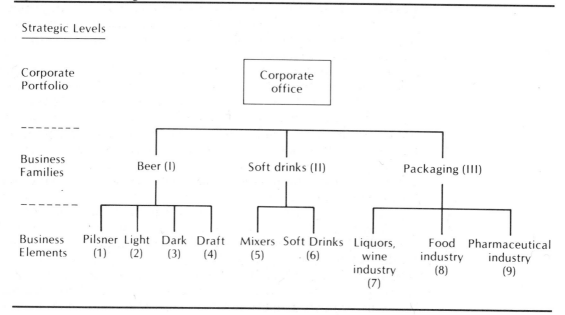

Strategic Levels

Corporate
Portfolio
Corporate office

- - - - - - -

Business
Families
Beer (I)   Soft drinks (II)   Packaging (III)

- - - - - -

Business
Elements
Pilsner (1)   Light (2)   Dark (3)   Draft (4)   Mixers (5)   Soft Drinks (6)   Liquors, wine industry (7)   Food industry (8)   Pharmaceutical industry (9)

for which the business's competitive position can also be established relative to specific competitors. The *business families* consist of related business elements for which it would be difficult to carry out competitive strategies individually without assessing the impacts on the others. The marketplace may have important synergies (economies of scale), so that business elements can be viewed as "colors on the business family palette". There may also be internal organizational synergies (economies of scope) in, for example, R&D, production, and distribution. Business families are similar to what General Electric originally denoted strategic business units (SBUs) (i.e., freestanding businesses that, in principle, can be sold off) (Vancil 1982).

The major motivation behind the introduction of the strategic structure was to strengthen the firm's ability to adapt to environmental opportunities by formulating and implementing more realistic competitive strategies. At the same time, still essential was maintaining the efficiency-oriented focus reflected in the operating structure; for this reason, a reorganization would be undesirable. Hence, *both* the strategic and the operating structures would have to be in effect. The control process was used as a major vehicle for integrating the strategic and the operating dimensions. It is important to remember that both strategic programs and budgets will be carried out today with a view to attaining their longer range purposes. It is easy for a casual observer to confuse such immediate steps with the ongoing tactical and operational activities. This aspect is elaborated on next.

Figure 4.7 illustrates the interlinked tasks of controlling strategic programs and strategic budgets. Let us specifically focus on the beer business family and two of its business elements: light and dark (see Figure 4.6). Light beer is a new business element that is in the process of being introduced. The objective is to develop a position for this beer in the higher-income younger consumer segment. Three strategic programs have been identified to attempt to achieve this objective: (1) the formulation of a new light beer, involving the brewing and beer-marketing operating divisions (consumer taste testing); (2) the development of an appropriate bottle and packaging, involving beer marketing, glass manufacturing, closures, and the carton plant as well as brewing (for usefully incorporating a new bottle dimension in the tapping plant); and (3) the actual launch, involving the beer marketing, brewing, glass-manufacturing, and distribution divisions. Dark beer is an old, well-established beer, which has traditionally been perceived by consumers as a nutritious drink. The objective is to relaunch and reposition the dark beer to render it appealing to the mature beer drinker who prefers a heavy-bodied beer. The strategic program that has been launched to achieve this objective involves beer marketing (to carry out a media campaign) and brewing (to develop a revised beer formulation and to prepare for production).

Control of the continued relevance of the objective requires following critical environmental assumptions. For light beer, an important step would be to continue to assess the growth potential for this business in terms of the extent to which consumers' preferences are moving in this direction. Also, one would want to monitor factors that might possibly dampen this growth, such as governmental taxation or other regulatory moves (or both). To monitor the development of one's own competitive strength, continued testing of consumer preference relative to other beers might be carried out. Relative market share might also give an indication of the strength position. Entry or exit (or both) of other brands must also be followed.

Various control tasks take place along both the strategic and the operating dimensions shown in Figure 4.7. Each strategic program needs to be controlled to ensure its progress toward preestablished milestones. For instance, the new beer formulation program (number 1 in Figure 4.7) will have to pass intermediary targets for completing initial forumlation in the laboratory, limited scale consumer taste testing, pilot scale batch brewing, full-scale consumer taste

Figure 4.7 *Compilation of Types of Strategic Control Variables (From Lorange 1984, 258)*

Two objectives, to be implemented by means of four strategic programs. This leads to derived strategic tasks for six departments. Three types of control tasks arise; vis-à-vis each objective, each strategic program, and each department's strategic budget.

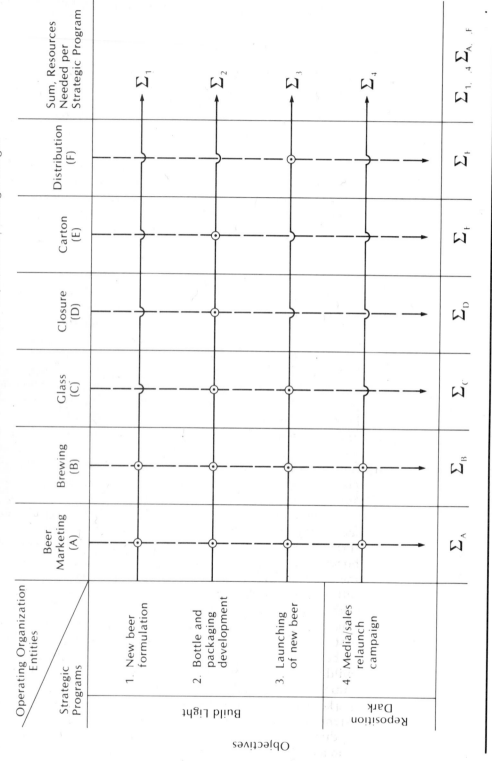

and appearance testing, and full-scale trial brewing. The calendar must also be followed to assess whether stages are completed on time. Similarly, resource spending per stage, broken down on each of the various departments, must be checked. Finally, relevant environmental assumptions must be monitored: Do the customer target groups seem to appreciate the light beer concept? If not, can the concept be modified? Are there indications that one or more competitors might also be preparing a light beer? If so, what actions might be taken? Does the approval of the new beer generate problems with the Food and Drug Administration? If so, what response should be made? The second aspect of the control of each strategic program deals with the resource usage pattern: Has time been spent and have costs been incurred in such a way that each department is doing its part of the overall team task? Although one must control for overspending, control for underspending is equally important in this context. The latter may signal that one or more functional entities are not tooled up to carry out their strategic assignments; day-to-day pressures may be occupying all their capacity.

The strategic budget of each operating division must also be controlled. Let us take the glass division as an example. We see from Figure 4.7 that this division is involved in two strategic programs, namely to carry out the strategic tasks of developing a new beer bottle as part of program 2 and to initiate new bottle production as part of program 3. Monitoring the spending of the resources provided in the strategic budget is necessary to establish that these funds are *not* used for operating purposes or "firefighting" in the the glass plant. Also, the monitoring should check to make sure that *both* strategic tasks are being pursued as intended.

Let us now return to a more general discussion of some critical factors underlying the delineation of objectives and implementation through strategic programs when it comes to highly interrelated businesses (i.e., at the so-called business family level). We recall that the creation of synergies is critical in this context. At the objective-setting stage, two sets of factors should definitely be monitored, both relating to critical assumptions underlying whether intended synergies between several business strategies can be achieved. The first is whether the market will allow synergies of any significance to be achieved: To what extent is there a realistic possibility of building up an overall broad recognition of, for instance, a brand name or a multibusiness umbrella theme? To what extent does the market show a need for a bundle of interrelated products? To what extent is there a market for a systems approach where a number of products are marketed together as part of a broader system rather than as separate items? The creation of such synergies often requires changes in the distribution system. The nature of such changes and their timing are critical questions. Discovering indicators that provide early signals that certain business elements can be put together in new and profitable ways can be particularly valuable. Similarly, spotting such attempted moves by existing and new competitors is critical. As a case in point we have seen that synergy creation has figured prominently in newly deregulated industries, such as banking and communications.

Second, environmental assumptions may influence whether internal synergies can be created to achieve benefits from horizontal and vertical integration and so on. External assumptions that might trigger internal synergies may relate to such diverse factors as changes in regulatory requirements, raw materials supply or transportation technology (or both), technological process changes, attitudinal changes in the human resource dimensions such as common views on multinationals, and so on.

With regard to strategic programs, competitor responses to synergistic types of strategies should be analyzed. Are competitors trying to meet the synergy-seeking strategy head-on; or are they trying to find weak spots in the business family strategy and attack these in a focused fashion? Similarly, customers' acceptance of an overall umbrella concept, such as the introduction of a common system, a common brand name profile, and so forth, should be reviewed. Finally, technology-based activities aimed at developing more broad-based efficiencies in manufacturing and distribution should be monitored.

Let us illustrate with an example some key strategic control issues relating to the monitoring of synergies between several businesses. A major manufacturer of ferroalloys was faced with the question of how to create synergies between several of its businesses, particularly between the ferrosilicon and the ferromanganese businesses. Both sets of products were manufactured by the company in question. Traditionally, the products had been sold to traders (i.e., treated as commodities). The company had observed that basic steel production was shifting to developing countries, such as Brazil, and Korea, while the specialty steel industry had gained relative importance in highly industrial countries, such as the United States and Europe. The company decided to develop its own marketing organization and to differentiate it to reach each particular growth segment. A special sales organization was created for certain countries to go after the specialty steel firms. In addition, the company was considering complementing the product spectrum with products such as ferrochromium, ferrovanadium, and ferromolybdenum, all purchased from other producers, to offer a full line of ferroalloys products.

To determine the optimal timing of this change, several critical environmental assumptions were monitored. First, the speed and magnitude of the shift in steel manufacturing were carefully followed. In particular, it was ascertained which steel manufacturers were becoming speciality steel producers in their entirety, thereby having a particular need for a full product package. Second, the cost-benefit ratio to particular customers was assessed: What, if anything, would a customer gain from having a full set of products, guaranteed for quality, stored and available at any point in time, relative to separate purchases of bulk quantities from traders at the risk of changing qualities and stockouts? This assessment of the relative cost benefits for the major set of potential customers guided the phasing in of the implementation of a market-based synergy strategy.

Let us now discuss the monitoring of critical environmental factors at the corporate portfolio level, relative to both objectives and strategic programs. What are the key variables at this strategic level?

With regard to objectives, key variables might include critical underlying factors behind the choice of intended optimal level of debt service, the chosen dividend service policy, the policy followed for taking economic and political risks, and so on. Such factors may be grounded in an overall economic outlook, in the economic conditions the particular sectors within which the company is operating, changes in the stock market's expectations regarding dividends, shifts in the political climate that might affect taxation, currency regulation, and so on. It is, for instance, important for management to monitor changes in owners' expectations regarding dividends: Are there any shifts in attitude on the part of the investment community in connection with what is typically seen as the normal level of expected return on invested capital? For instance, several companies have been taken over by unfriendly suitors at least in part as a result of top management's insufficient attention to the value-creation expectations of its stock holders. The stock price may have remained relatively low while the hidden values of the company might have increased. Too much may have been reinvested in the company and too little paid out as dividends, thus creating an attractive takeover target. Lack of sensitivity to changes in the general stockholder attitude toward expected value generation may cause such takeover attempts.

Critical factors that might impact strategic programs at the corporate level would include those relating to when and how to make a divestiture or an acquisition (or both), such as reactions from potential sellers and buyers, the stockmarket, and the cost of capital. Such divestitures or acquisitions (or both) may be crucial for implementing a more active shareholder value-creation approach.

In determining whether to sell off a particular part of the company, another variable to be assessed would be the potential disruptive effect on the remaining parts of the company's operation, overhead structure, and so on. Similarly, when acquiring a new business, it is necessary to assess whether one's assumptions regarding the cost effects of integrating such a business actually hold. Strategic programs for corporate R&D and corporate venturing may also be influenced by variable environmental factors.

The prior examples illustrate how to identify critical environmental factors in one's search for a comprehensive understanding of the forces affecting the development of an objective or a strategic program (or both) and how various sources of environmental factors might have impacts. Such a delineation must be specific to a given strategic setting. The key is to focus on a set of factors that are seen to be highly critical to such an extent that they can be understood and monitored by the organization. The incorporation of such factors in the control system adds to the forward-forward capabilities of the control system beyond what can be achieved by merely monitoring deviations from intended performance along traditional output measures.

We still need classical responsibility center control. It is not an either-or situation. The need also exists for another type of complementary strategic momentum control, which involves questioning whether the basic strategic momentum as a whole is still valued. The alternative answer to such a question would be that there might be time to shift toward another strategy by means of a strategic leap. What is needed, in other words, is a way of judging when to shift from strategic momentum control to the strategic leap control mode. We approach this challenge of becoming sensitized to when there is need to consider a strategic leap by means of controlling the continued relevance of the basic generic strategies followed through the strategic momentum, the topic discussed in the next section. In Chapter 5, then, we shall return to a full-pledged discussion of strategic leap control.

GENERIC STRATEGY: CHECKING AND TESTING

A third type of strategic momentum control is checking the basic strategies being pursued to determine whether they seem to be reasonable or normal relative to what one would expect, either based on information collected empirically on the status of other similar strategies in comparable corporations or by reviewing the appropriateness of such strategies in a particular type of competitive environment. We shall denote this strategic control relative to generic strategies. Before outlining the pros and cons of this approach, we briefly pay proper attention to the pioneering work of Professor Michael Porter in developing generic strategies (Porter 1980) and describe two types of generic strategies, one empirically derived and one normatively developed.

The empirically derived generic strategy approach stems primarly from the data-based approach developed by the Strategic Planning Institute, often denoted PIMS (Profit Impact of Market Strategy) (Schoeffler, Buzzell, and Heaney 1974). Over a number of years, more than two thousand businesses have been reporting their strategies and their particular situational settings along a number of dimensions. This information has enabled researchers to identify which particular strategic approaches are optimal to gain a better strategic result, such as higher return on investment, higher market share, or higher profits. A particular business can thereby compare itself to the norm experienced by other firms in connection with evaluating such strategic decisions as R&D intensity, market expenses, and new product and process innovations. This might help a firm to see if its contemplated strategy is at odds with the norm. Similarly, corporations can use the data-based program to identify ways to improve their strategy so as to encourage relatively higher performance.

The strategic control benefit from this approach is that one gets a rough verification as to whether one's strategy is basically in line with the norm. It might indicate that a corporation's strategy is not one that usually yields a strategic advantage or that it deviates sharply from the norm, causing management to think through why it is following such a seemingly unorthodox approach. Nothing is wrong with doing business differently from others, of course, as long as one realizes why an alternate direction is being pursued. The most successful business strategies are often those that do not follow the average.

This suggests a seemingly basic limitation with generic strategy testing via the PIMS approach: There is no one "right" generic strategy. The PIMS data reflect the average performance of a number of strategies compiled by different companies, nothing more, nothing less. They do not indicate in any absolute sense what is right or wrong, and strategies other than the ones indicated by PIMS may well be better. These performance data can, however, serve as a good initial basis for reexamining one's own strategic direction regarding its degree of conformity with the PIMS data-base patterns.

Several conceptually related approaches are the normative frameworks developed by Henderson (1979), Arthur D. Little (1974), MacMillan (1982), and others which indicate the strategic approach a particular business should take during the various stages of its product life cycle (from start-up to maturity), and when it is a leader versus a follower in each of these stages. For instance, Henderson (1979) suggests what would be an appropriate strategy under four different situational competitive settings: when experiencing high growth in the business but a relatively low market share ("question mark" strategy), when experiencing high growth and enjoying a high relative market share ("star" strategy), when faced with a relatively low growth business rate but enjoying high market share ("cash cow" strategy), and finally, when facing both relatively low business growth and a low relative market share ("dog" strategy). Four different categories of market share thrusts have been defined to fit in this situation, being the natural, or generic, strategies of build, hold, harvest, and withdraw or divest. The Arthur D. Little (1974) approach suggests the optimal strategy when moving from start-up toward maturity—when emphasis shifts from product innovations to process innovations, from R&D intensity to cost efficiency, from market differentiation toward more standardized market approaches. The approach also indicates how to build, sustain, and manage a withdrawal from a particular business segment at each stage of maturity. By profiling one's businesses, one can determine whether the strategies are consistent with what they normatively should be according to this scheme. Arthur D. Little has grouped its generic strategies into six major categories, which emphasize their major purpose for strategic development: marketing strategies, integration strategies, go overseas strategies, logistics strategies, efficiency strategies, and harvest strategies. MacMillan (1982) has proposed a set of generic strategies, which fall into eight different categories: build aggressively, build gradually, build selectively, maintain aggressively, maintain selectively, prove viability, divest/liquidate, and competitive harasser.

These approaches may provide opportunity for broad checkups of one's strategies, and represent verification of strategic momentum control that can be useful. These generic strategies, however, are limited in the same way as the empirically derived strategies: namely, there is no one "correct" generic strategy. This form of strategic control can only sensitize the management to whether it is departing from what has been established as a reasonable approach and if so, whether its reasons are valid. The purpose of checking one's strategies according to generic dimensions regarding basic soundness and logic, as briefly indicated previously, involves getting overall verification of whether the basic strategic momentum and its underlying strategy are still plausible. One might of course also get signals that the underlying strategy is no longer valid from the other types of strategic momentum control, notably when the critical success factors no longer seem to hold or when major problems occur in responsibility center control. Beyond this, however, a useful approach is to take an overall view of the generic soundness and intuitive relevance of one's strategies, again getting indications that it may be time to fundamentally reexamine these strategies by means of a strategic leap approach.

THE INCREMENTAL NATURE
OF STRATEGIC MOMENTUM CONTROL

The incremental management process model was built, piece by piece, from the research of many authors who noted that the actual behavior of organizations and managers was often based on a trial-and-error approach. These observations include:

- the findings of Baybrooke and Lindbloom (1963) that observed decisions of organizations resemble far more a pattern of muddling through than a purposeful movement from one point to another;
- the important role of internal power dynamics in shaping organizational decisions in terms of what is politically acceptable and feasible has been observed by, Cyert, Simon, and Trow (1956), Bower (1970), Zalesnik, and Kets de Vries (1975), Allison (1971), and Pettigrew (1973);
- Mintzberg's (1973) observation that a manager's work bears little resemblance to the traditional categorization of functions such as planning, organizing, staffing, directing, coordinating, reporting, and budgeting. Instead, a manager works relentlessly at a series of small tasks, and activity is characterized by brevity, variety, and fragmentation.

Quinn (1980) has developed an integrated approach based on the previous theoretical perspectives and proposed a model of strategic management that he calls "logical incrementalism."

As pointed out before, the closed-loop feedback control systems, as exemplified by the three classes of momentum control discussed earlier in this chapter, are forms of control consistent with such incrementalism. Similarly, classical strategic planning approaches carried out on an annual basis can be seen as another form of incrementalism. We shall therefore now find it useful to elaborate on the incrementalism concept as a way of summarizing some of the key features of strategic momentum control. What is important to note in Quinn's argument is the justification of incrementalism regarding both cognitive and process limits of subsystems. The process limits are often ignored even in more modern and behaviorally oriented views of strategic control. Logical incrementalism further supports our basic argument that strategic planning and strategic control are simultaneous interacting processes—two sides of the same coin. Implementation and control are the chief rationale for incrementalism. The control areas highlighted by incrementalism are the "soft" issues usually ignored in most models of strategic planning. Quinn especially emphasizes the importance of informal and bypass communication channels as essential to proactive management of the incremental process. Through these channels, top management is sensitized to emerging issues. He argues:

> Successful enterprises, of course, have many formally structured horizon scanning, planning, and reporting systems to alert them to pending changes, but rarely in my observations did the earliest signals for strategic change come from these sources. Instead, they appeared in highly diffuse and informal ways. Seldom did a manager immediately know what precise action—if any—a complex issue called for. Rather, as one high level observer noted, "At this stage our top people spent a lot of time talking in the halls, asking questions for clarification, bringing in new information sources, and trying to sort out what was really relevant." Top executives themselves frequently described initially need sensing in the following terms: "something you felt uneasy about," "a general feeling that we needed to do something new," or "we could all see a problem developing, but didn't know what it meant or precisely what to do." (Quinn 1980, 107)

Another important control device is the manipulation of symbols. Symbols and symbolic actions are used not only to establish the credibility of a new strategy but also to send silent messages about changing flux in the organization. Still another important control mechanism in incrementalism is legitimizing. The primary and ultimate instrument of legitimizing is empowering champions. A basic rationale of incrementalism is to cope with uncertainty; thus, the validity of the original strategy lies not in whether it maintained intact but in its capacity to adapt successfully to unknowable realities, reshape itself, and ultimately use resources most effectively toward selected goals. Under such circumstances, control against predeterimined performance measure is no longer possible, and manager-management and decision context management (see pages 96–97) become the principal control mechanisms. This means that the right people to manage a given strategic thrust must be legitimized and empowerd, and also that the reward system must be tailored to support the given strategic thrust.

An emerging concept of integrated strategic management that bridges the transition from strategic momentum to strategic leap control has been offered by Hax and Majluf (1984) in their summarization of many key ideas in the field. Strategic management in their view is essentially an eclectic concept that ties together at least three major dimensions:

1. A set of powerful analytical tools for designing strategy at the levels of a business, a business family, and the total corporation. At the business level the techniques include exploiting the experience curve and the industry and competitive analysis framework of Porter (1980). At the business family level, the key concept is segmentation (i.e., the identification of SBUs based on, among others, the conept of the value-added chain with optimum use of economy of scale within each value component and economy of scope across the components). At the corporate level, the tools include various approaches to the portfolio matrix, including the growth-share matrix of the Boston Consulting Group (Henderson 1979), the industry attractiveness–business strength matrix developed jointly by General Electric and McKinsey (Rotschild 1980), and the life cycle portfolio matrix developed by Arthur D. Little (1974). Recently, another set of powerful tools has been added to this array: the market to book value model that attempts to integrate finance with strategy through the concept of value creation. Examples of this are the profitability matrix developed by Marakon Associates, Inc. (1980), the Shareholder Value Curve developed by Strategic Planning Associates (1984), and a somewhat related approach developed by Rappaport (1981).

2. Methods for integrating the strategic management system with other organizational systems, such as the control system, the information and communication system, as well as the incentive and reward system.

3. Techniques for evolving a fit between strategy and organizational culture so as to prevent incompatibility and keep cultural rejection risks within acceptable levels.

Our objective is not to discuss these dimensions in further detail or to describe the different tools and techniques more than already done. From our point of view, however, it is interesting to note a seemingly emerging consensus that integrated strategic management provides a powerful set of analytical tools which, when tied together with a good organizational process, can yield significant benefits. We shall elaborate further on this in Chapter 5.

MECHANISMS OF STRATEGIC MOMENTUM CONTROL

Many researchers have conducted research on how the tasks of coordination and control are exercised in one of the most complex forms of diversified organizations, the diversified multinationals.

Based on their study of ten large multinational corporations, Doz and Prahalad (1981) identified three such types of strategic control mechanisms that may be available to corporate-level managers.

- *Data management mechanisms.* Data management mechanisms are those such as information systems, measurement systems, resource allocation procedures, and strategic planning and budgeting processes, through which corporate managers receive information about divisional performance and can control strategic behavior through the allocation of corporate resources. Principally, they are tools for control through formalizing the patterns of dependencies between the headquarters and its business entities.

- *Manager management mechanisms.* Manager management mechanisms are processes such as selection, socialization, and rewards and punishments, through which corporate managers can influence subunit behaviors by controlling the behavior of key personnel.

- *Conflict resolution mechanisms.* Conflict resolution mechanisms are for creating strategic and administrative integration among subunits through the creation of communication channels and formal and informal processes that facilitate the development of shared understanding of both corporate- and subunit-level challenges, aspirations, goals, and strategies.

Bartlett (1979) suggests that these mechanisms used individually and collectively lead to three different modes of strategic control.

- *Control through substantive decision management.* In the first mode, control is exercised by direct involvement of corporate managers in the decision processes. They receive different, often polarized, perspectives from the divisional managers who represent the division's view and corporate staff managers who act as in-house auditors of those views that represent the corporate-level interests.

■ *Control through temporary coalition management.* The substantive decision management mode suffers from a number of potential shortcomings. First, as noted, views as they are reported to top management may tend to be polarized, often reflecting extreme perspectives rather than balanced judgments. Second, it may generate excessive demands on top management time. Finally, it may lead to implementation difficulties, since managers representing the "losing" side may tend to become less than enthusiastic about implementing decisions they so recently may have opposed so strongly.

Such problems may lead to the evolution of what Bartlett calls the temporary coalition management mode. Integrative mechanisms such as task forces, teams, and committees are created to synthesize the different perspectives. As these mechanisms are used, managers with different views and concerns may learn to work better together so as to either arrive at a consensus or at least focus issues before escalating them to higher organizational levels. Senior corporate managers can, to a greater or lesser extent, delegate decision making to such temporary structures and coalitions and yet maintain some strategic control over the decision process by being able to set the agenda for the teams, impact the composition of the temporary groups, and select the leadership of such think tank structures.

■ *Control through decision context management.* Even the temporary coalition management mode has its limitations. Often, such team structures may degenerate into forced alliances between reluctant colleagues, leading to horse trading or even paralysis of the decision process. Besides, even this mode may make heavy demands on top management time and energy for forming, restructuring, and dissolving temporary coalitions to manage an often growing number of multidimensional problems. The result may be a degeneration of decision-making drive due to excessive time and energy spent on ad hoc committees.

These constraints lead to the adoption of what can be labeled decision context management—a mode in which intensive formal and informal communication among managers, a shared perspective developed through rotation and transfer of managers, and an institutionalized value system supporting constructive and cooperative interactions are brought together to achieve and maintain a self-regulating and flexible decision process.

Barlett describes these modes in an evolutionary model in which substantive decision management leads to temporary coalition management, which in turn evolves into decision context management as the organization matures and its strategic control systems develop. Perhaps more useful would be to consider the three modes as components of the strategic control system in diversified firms—components that coexist with different degrees of emphasis on one or the other under different circumstances.

A CONTINGENCY FRAMEWORK FOR PEACETIME STRATEGIC CONTROL

As indicated in the discussion in this chapter, it is critical that a particular organization be controlled along several dimensions in its peacetime mode. The synthesis of these dimensions, seen together, provides signals for executive action. Figure 4.8 summarized the major individual components of peacetime strategic control approaches that we have discussed, and provides a summary of the types of emphasis that should characterize the strategic momentum control of the various types of corporations delineated within the table. Figure 4.8 thus serves as a summary of our approach to strategic momentum control, suggesting that firms that resemble any particular category of strategic value generation need to employ a combination of any four strategic momentum approaches, indicated in the table by the horizontal array of encircled approaches next to each of the three examples of firms. It is the interpretation and synthesis of such a combined set of control signals that is the key to effective strategic momentum control. The critical managerial challenge in this context is to be able to make the appropriate judgment calls based on a balanced reconciliation of a multitude of signals.

Figure 4.8   Compilation of Types of Strategic Control Variables

	Controlling of ...			
Examples of Strategic Values-Generation Approaches	Key Variables Underlying Objectives	Key Variables Underlying Strategic Programs	Strategic Budgets	Operating Budgets
I. Companies that Emphasize Value-Added Chain Forward-Backward Integration	① The viability of the product-market niche ■ growth ■ strength	② ■ Coordinated new products competitor's reactions customer's responses ■ Vertical integration synergies	③ ■ For new products ■ For vertical integration (Discretionary items in cost and revenue centers)	④ ■ Cost Centers ■ Revenue Centers
II. Companies that Emphasize Synergies via Economies of Scope or Scale (or both)	⑤ The viability of the business family ■ market synergies ■ internal synergies [Also ①]	⑥ ■ Coordinated market systems competitor's reactions customer's responses [Also ②]	⑦ ■ For market systems ■ For internal synergies [Also ③]	⑧ Profit Centers [Also ④]
III. Companies that Emphasize Corporate-wide Value Creation	⑨ The viability of the portfolio ■ shareholder value [Also ①]	⑩ Acquisitions and Divestitures Internal Diversification [Also ②]	⑪ ■ Internal Development	⑫ Investment Centers

5

Understanding Discontinuity: Strategic Leap Control

INTRODUCTION

In the previous chapter, we reviewed the concepts of strategic control as they arise from classical views of strategic planning. Recently, increasing concern has been expressed by many prominent authors in the field that these methods focus too closely on the analysis of the strategic problem under relatively stable, well-understood conditions and not enough on the organizational process through which strategic decisions emerge during more turbulent, discontinuity-driven times. In such periods, strategic decision situations are "messy" and involve unstructured problems and ambiguity that linear methods of strategic planning and control cannot effectively address (Chaffe 1985). We also argued in the introductory chapter of this book that these classical methods implicitly assume environmental continuity and are oriented more toward evolving strategies than toward analysis of the types of key strategic assumptions that might indicate major shifts and discontinuities in strategic direction. Our conclusion in the previous chapter was that these methods are necessary but not sufficient for a modern system of strategic control appropriate to this era of discontinuities.

In this chapter, we review a number of more recent methods for strategic planning that we collectively labeled in Chapter 1 as wartime approaches to reflect their special sensitivity to possible environmental discontinuities. These methods have not yet suffered from overexposure as have some of the more classical methods. On the contrary, general awareness about these strategic control tools is perhaps less than what is desirable. We briefly describe the salient features of the different methods and articulate their implications for strategic control. We focus on four approaches: strategic issue management, strategic field analysis, systems modeling, and scenario planning.

We emphasize that this chapter discusses approaches to planning and related control in times of considerable changes—times that may call for discontinuous leaps by the organization. In no way are these methods better than the more classical methods; they are simply different and are appropriate for use at different times.

STRATEGIC ISSUE MANAGEMENT

In the 1970s a backlash occurred against strategic planning on the grounds that at times it tended to become too shallow and that truly critical issues might easily be overlooked in annual repetitive assessments of the multiple strategies of the firm. A belief emerged that no organization can successfully manage more than one or two major issues at a time. This led to the concept of single-issue planning, where the organization identifies one or a few key issues that are believed crucial for achieving its performance objectives. The organization directs its collective energy toward understanding the impact of the issue and in overcoming the threats or exploiting the opportunities posed by the issue. The issue may be either forced upon the organization (such as government deregulation in the airline business) or adopted by the organization, usually through a declaration by the board or by the CEO. As an example of the latter, the chairman of General Motors may declare that to remain the world's largest automobile manufacturer, GM must deal with the issues of productivity and quality. Having declared a strategic issue, the organization turns its attention to solving it and, in a well-run organization, establishes criteria for success and measures itself against them. Thus, the issue-based approach lends itself readily to wartime strategic control. This is not surprising in that the issue or issues are already focused to some degree and are identified based on their perceived effect on performance. Thus, the objectives to be achieved can clearly be stated. Significant milestones can also usually be established, facilitating the control process.

The concept of single-issue management has recently been broadened in the form of strategic issues management (Ansoff 1980) and strategic issues analysis (King 1982). These have been modeled as processes and systems designed to be flexible, sensitive, and action oriented, thereby minimizing the probability and reducing the impact of strategic surprises. Essentially, the Strategic Issues Management System (SIMS) has been proposed as an alternative approach to the Strategic Planning System (SPS). The differences between the two systems have been summarized by Camillus and Datta (1984) as follows:

1. Most SPS's are based on periodic activities, while SIMs by their very nature have to be continuous in character. An SPS usually involves a process of scanning, analysis and strategy formulation that is normally repeated at pre-set intervals. The SIMS by contrast is event rather than time-triggered and consequently is a constantly ongoing process.

2. The conventional SPS tends to respond to "strong" signals, while SIMS is intended to pick up "weak," not so obvious signals.

3. As a corollary of (1) and (2) above, the SPS focuses on issues directly relatable to the organization itself while the SIMS presumably is receptive to issues emanating from any source. Furthermore, it is suggested that the SPS itself is somewhat narcissistic in character in that executing the process of planning becomes the superordinate goal.

4. The output of the SPS is typically characterized by a vision of what the organization would aspire to be and to achieve; the SIMS in contrast endeavors to ascertain the pragmatic consequences of identified issues and focuses on actions to reduce the negative impacts of or exploit the opportunities offered by strategic discontinuities.

5. The orientation of the SPS towards the existing organization and the emphasis on enacting a predetermined process normally results in analysis and outputs that are significantly influenced by the status quo, the existing structure and power relationships (Bower 1970; Prahalad 1976). In contradistinction the task forces envisaged by Ansoff (1975) and King and Cleland (1978) orient the SIMS to non-traditional modes of thought and action.

6. Finally, given the goal orientation suggested in (4) above, the SPS would be biased towards a goals-means sequence in strategy formulation. The SIMS, however, given its ad hoc, essentially reactive character, would inherently be limited to a means-goals sequence. The paucity of related information characteristic of "weak" signals would reinforce this intrinsic orientation of the SIMS.

Evidence indicates that senior-level practitioners have shown visible interest in SIMS. In two recent Conference Board monographs, Brown (1979, 1981) has discussed the implementation of strategic issues analysis in organizations such as AT&T, PPG Industries, GE, American Council of Life Insurance, Shell, and Sun Oil. The driving concern behind the adaptation of strategic issues management is the need for early-early warning signals discussed in Chapter 4. This is clear from a statement of the Environmental Research Group at GE: "Without proper response societal expectations of today become the political issues of tommorrow, legislated requirements the next day and the litigated penalties the day after that" (Brown 1981, 6).

A highly successful example of strategic issues analysis fulfilling this early-early warning role is the Trend Analysis Program (TAP) of the American Council of Life Insurance, which "helps member company decisions by anticipating legislative resolutions, *sensitizing* executives to changing public needs and enunciating issues (as formulated by a creative elite) *before* they reached the public agenda, thereby allowing a longer lead time for formulating strategies" (Camillus and Datta 1984, 6) (emphasis added). The key word here is *sensitizing*, which we have proposed in Chapter 2 as the crucial first step to successful strategic change. This emphasis on sensitizing is also manifest in the description of a Sun Oil executive of how the large energy firm manages strategic change through a "Future Issues Committee" (Weiss 1978). The committee is a freewheeling group, operating in an unstructured fashion. It consists of representatives from the environmental assessment group, an officer from human resources, representatives from government affairs, and the vice-chairman of the company. The objective of the committee is to identify and sensitize the organization to emerging issues of interest—from the fuzzy to the concrete—well before their impacts are directly visible either in performance measures or even in the specific task environment.

An important implication of strategic issues management for strategic control is suggested by Dutton and Duncan (1984), who suggest that one must be cognizant of the strategic issues array, which is defined as the set of strategic issues consuming the attention of decision makers. This set has a number of characteristics:

Array size	Number of different strategic issues in the array
Array variety	Diversity of issues included in the array
Array turnover	Frequency of issues moving into and out of the array
Issue scope	Breadth of the issue domain covered by an issue

Too large an array size creates impediments both for the initiation of strategic change and for its implementation. At the initiation stage, multiple issues vie for attention, both reflecting and supporting the political agendas of members. A large array also creates problems of information overload. At the implementation stage, change burnouts and excessive informational demands make strategic control difficult to achieve. Similarly, large issue variety causes difficulties in obtaining consensus and commitments, and leads to fragmentation of efforts and resources. On the other hand, rapid issue turnover along with small array size can promote initiation of change by the perception that action will be taken, and broad issue scope can make implementation effective by obtaining a broader base of commitment.

Given these effects of array size and diversity on the initiation and implementation of strategic change, the conclusion, from the point of strategic control, is a vote in favor of a simple, relatively informal top-down planning process that focuses intensively on a few critical issues at a time, thus concentrating the psychological and physical resources of the organization on an effort to achieve well-defined change objectives. The major challenge is therefore to identify the critical issues that should be the subject of the organization's all-encompassing analysis. By not being sufficiently selective and by focusing on too many issues, the purpose of in-depth analysis is refuted. Also, by focusing on a less than critical issue, the benefits of the analysis might be less than what would be merited given the efforts. Top management must be critically involved in choosing the key issue for analysis.

The wartime strategic control challenge is to examine the critical issues from all angles and to thereby identify new opportunities from the insights gained. Executives each see a problem or phenomenon through their own "mental lenses"—shaped by their education as well as by their experience and background. Certain dimensions of a problem can therefore be more easily understood than any other dimensions by particular individuals, depending on their expertise. By bringing together executives with different, possibly complementary backgrounds, one might hope to achieve an overall picture of the phenomenon, a more holistic in-depth understanding of the issue at hand. Thus, eclecticism, multiple viewpoints, exchanges between executives who see things in different ways, and so on are essential ingredients of this form of wartime strategic control. Overly inbred executive groups, highly structured so as to prevent viewpoints from being raised in a free-flowing manner and conditioned so as to avoid raising disagreements, would be dysfunctional in relation to this form of strategic control.

STRATEGIC FIELD ANALYSIS

Strategic field analysis is a simplified way of directing attention to the nature and extent of synergies that exist—or do not exist—between the components of an organization. It consists of two aspects. One is to analyze the value-added chain in terms of the various functional steps involved in providing a particular business output. For instance, a particular functional step would be to identify the costs that are to be offset against the overall selling price for the product. Stated differently, what would be lost if a particular functional step were not performed in-house but contracted through an outside party?

The second dimension of strategic field analysis consists of examining potential synergies between the various products, markets, or businesses—for instance, by taking advantage of joint manufacturing or a coordinated marketing approach. That is, one examines the potential benefits of synergies among the various business companies involved for each of the functional areas. Let us now discuss each of these two steps in strategic field analysis in more detail.

The Value-Added Chain and Potential Synergies

The concept of industry value-added chains that is emerging from the discipline of industrial economics is a powerful way to visualize the nature of value creation within a business and to identify the leverage points that it offers for building up competitive advantages. Important contributions to this approach have recently been made by Porter (1985), Kogut (1984), and others.

The value-added chain depicts the discrete activities in which a firm must engage to produce and market a product or service. The concept of a value-added chain is generic and can be constructed for any industry by differentiating the activity components that have different inherent economies—those that can at least be partially decoupled. They should also be significant contributors to cost or else add value in significant ways, such as being important for differentiation. Each value element (say, advertising or distribution) has an inherent scale economy. Scope economies are also present both within a value element (e.g., transfer of learning from one production plant to another) and across value elements (e.g., the knowledge of efficient use of task forces acquired in the production function and subsequently used in the marketing function). A typical value-added chain is shown in Figure 5.1.

Strategic field analysis visualizes the many businesses of a diversified firm in terms of the different value-added chains and the nature of scale and scope benefits that can be obtained from their overlap. This is done by developing a strategic field map showing the chains for the businesses and how synergies between these business value chains can be developed.[1] Figure 5.2 shows a highly sim-

1. To our knowledge, this technique was first used in practice by Strategic Planning Associates (SPA, Inc.) in 1980.

Figure 5.1   A Typical Value-Added Chain

Research and Development						
Procurement						
Inbound logistics	Component fabrication	Assembly and tooling	Outbound logistics	Advertising and other marketing	Sales force	Service

Upstream value elements   Downstream value elements
Economies of scales dominated ⟵————————⟶ Economies of scope dominated

plified form of such a map for Procter and Gamble (Strategic Planning Associates 1981). The map clearly shows the mutual reinforcements that the different businesses of Procter and Gamble provide. It also indicates that animal feed ingredients stand almost isolated and are therefore not closely tied to the company's strategic field. From the viewpoint of direct synergy, it suggests that Procter and Gamble should carefully examine the relevance of the fit of this relatively unconnected business. It also reflects the high degree of fit inherent in P&G's acquisitions of Charmin, Duncan Hines, and Folger's.

This method promises to be a powerful wartime strategic control technique. At present it focuses only on shared operations, but it can easily be extended to review synergies in the areas of distinctive competence and shared images and values (see Chapter 6). Such an expanded strategic field analysis can permit managers to exercise strategic control by matching "actual" with "potential" and in so doing, discover new opportunities. Further, it can permit a more realistic assessment of competitive dynamics when diversified firms face each other in a range of businesses (see Porter [1985] for much more detailed treatment). The strategic field map offers management a way to control whether the basic gravity points in the company's value-creation process are properly focused. One can even conceive of dramatically changing the value-creating emphasis of the company, say, by adding new businesses, forging new synergies, changing the center of value-added for a set of businesses by integrating forward, and so on. The opportunities for major shifts in value creation can thus be exposed and the change process monitored.

Figure 5.2 Procter & Gamble Strategic Field (Reproduced with the permission of Strategic Planning Associates, Inc., 1981)

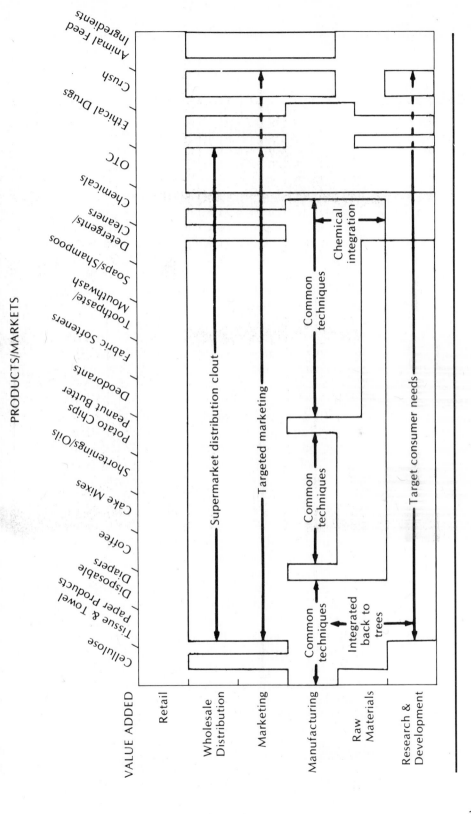

SYSTEMS MODELING

A strategic leap control effort requires two particular types of analysis, which typically come into play as soon as the rudiments of the discontinuous change have been delineated through strategic field analysis or strategic issues analysis or both. These two analytical efforts are necessary to generate a more in-depth systematic understanding of the interfaces between the strategy and the external and internal environments. The interface with the external environment will be dealt with primarily via scenario analysis, which is the topic of the next section. In this section, we discuss systems modeling as a vehicle to address the feasibility of options for strategic changes, given the internal organizational reality of the company. The emphasis is thus on ascertaining whether the particular strategies one might be contemplating are feasible and, if so, identifying the key dimensions for subsequent monitoring. This analysis helps to avoid unrealistic strategies and facilitates better coordination of various business programs, thus avoiding internal organizational inefficiencies.

The cost of developing such models, both in cost and in management time, is high. The effort should therefore not be made unless the potential payoff is high. Although in some instances, a major change has occurred in the context of peacetime conditions, such high payoff situations occur more frequently during discontinuous leaps into new domains. Thus, such models are most useful when used by management as a way of developing an understanding of the risks, rewards, and dynamics of making such a leap. The analysis process identifies the dimensions along which such a move needs to be monitored as part of a strategic control system. As suggested in the Introduction, there is a growing recognition of the need for such dynamic analysis.

Systems models can be developed in many ways. Typically, these computer-based models are focused on trying to capture the administrative realities of a particular organization and how it interfaces with its environment. The bounded rationality of the organization is modeled in an attempt to provide a behavioral description of the organization's policies and their interconnections, emphasizing feedback effects from various administrative actions.

Model building of this type has several characteristics among which are:

1. These models are typically "one-shot" entities. They are meant to illustrate how a particular dynamic strategy impacts an organization and vice versa, particularly what kinds of organizational

bottlenecks and shortages one might run into in terms of capacities, staffing, financial constraints, and so on. After this information is analyzed within the organization's particular wartime decision-making context and key variables are identified, the model is discarded.

2. The models are not necessarily elaborate. Typically, a situation is modeled, and then various modifications are introduced as management manipulates the model to generate better ways to describe the situation (see Figure 5.3).

3. The purpose of the modeling effort is to emphasize the sensitivities to which one should be particularly alert in assessing how robust an organization has to be when responding to various strategic options. It can also provide insight as to how one might correct various organizational shortcomings and avoid bottlenecks and similar problems that might otherwise surface as a result of pursuing a given strategy.

Thus, a fundamental approach is to look at systems modeling as an interactive strategic control approach, wherein management and model interface on a what-if basis to better understand the interplay between the internal environment and various dynamic strategies. A useful way of looking at the iterative modeling of this interplay has been developed by Morecroft and Paich (1984) (see Figure 5.3).

As can be seen in Figure 5.3, the procedure begins with a statement of one's initial understanding of the organization and market structure; this leads to a descriptive process model for the organization in its strategic setting. A delineation of a business policy and strategy for the organization is then derived, partly from one's initial understanding of the organizational context and partly from the clarification and understanding that result from developing the process model. The clarification of understanding has two stages. First, the process model becomes the basis for a mathematical model, which might be formalized by means of a system dynamics approach. Then, the mathematical process model is simulated to further understanding of the system's feedback structure and its dynamic behavior. The simulation analysis must be supplemented by graphics, decision support system, and low-cost computation. This iterative procedure continues until mangement is reasonably sure how a particular dynamic strategy might work relative to the internal environment of the firm.

We emphasize that systems modeling is not an optimization effort. Rather, it attempts to sensitize the management team to how a number of organizational dimensions may change in response to the dynamic development of a particular strategy. One of the challenges

Figure 5.3 Accumulating Knowledge of Model Structures for Use in the Analysis of Business Strategy (From Morecroft and Paich 1984, 16)

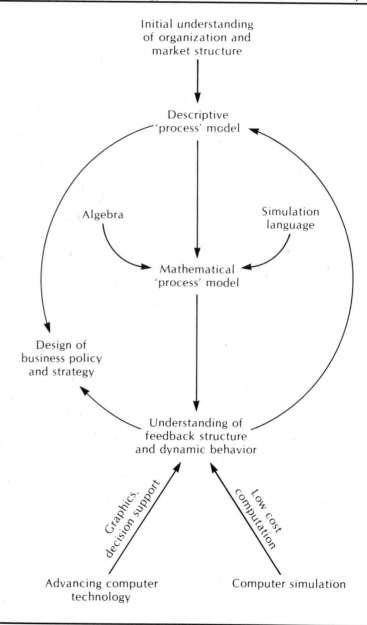

is to carry out such a systems modeling in such a way that the cognitive limitations of management are kept in mind. Management must be able to internalize what each of these sensitivity runs means relative to the others. The value of systems modeling is determined by the manager's ability to synthesize the information derived from such models.

One visible stream of work in the systems modeling area is system dynamics. Professor Jay Forrester fo the Sloan School at MIT (1981) is responsible for the development of this feedback flow model of organizations, and he argues that control should be heavily based on this concept. In his simulation of societal systems, Forrester (1981) maintains that complex systems

- are counterintuitive and remarkably insensitive to changes in many parameters.
- resist policy changes.
- contain influential pressure points from which to manage the system and improve its performance. These pressure points can often be found in unexpected places.
- react to externally applied pressures by adjusting internal interactions in directions opposite to the external pressures.
- react to policy changes in opposite ways in the long and short term.

All these findings have implications for strategic control. For example, an organization's short-term operating control can build up pressures generated through their short-term control process that can have the opposite effect from the one desired when viewed in a strategic context.

System dynamics demonstrates several important lessons applicable to strategic control. One is that control measures must not be seen in isolation as simple cause-and-effect relations. Rather, the broader long-term effects of ad hoc crisis-driven short-term control are often different from that anticipated and may conflict with the objectives of strategic control. A second implication is that system dynamics delineates particularly effective control levers that will impact and change the systems' behavior. This has direct applicability to strategic control, which seeks to identify and emphasize those factors that can give top management the best levers for impacting the direction of their organization and for developing more focused strategic control systems. Perhaps the broadest implication of system dynamics for our purpose is the need to see control of organizations in a dynamic context, with an understanding of the reasons for past direction and a sensitivity to the critical factors that seem likely to impact the future. As such, system dynamics provides strong support for the concept of developing a better understanding of key underlying success factors.

Besides system dynamics, other ways of developing systems models useful for strategic control. Professor Thomas H. Naylor of Duke University is well known for his work on corporate simulation models (Naylor 1979). His models use concepts from econometrics and operation management, instead of the behavioral decision theory and feedback theory in system dynamics. They therefore emphasize different features of organization and market structure. However, these models, too, offer a capability for interactive strategic control by allowing management and model to interface on the evaluation of strategic options.

For both momentum control and leap control, an important role is to be played by systems modeling. Extensive literature is available on the subject, some of the most important of which is listed in the References. However, the work of Naylor captures the best of the more accepted simulation work, and the work of those involved in system dynamics adds a dimension possibly unfamiliar to many readers.

SCENARIO-BASED STRATEGY DEVELOPMENT

Scenario planning has an evolutionary history that traces its antecedents back to future studies, which were pioneered, among others, by the Rand Corporation (e.g., Gordon and Helmer 1964) and which are still under active development by groups such as the World Futures Society. Such efforts involve examining broad sociopolitical trends, describing alternative major scenarios, and developing an assessment of which one is most likely. The importance of the scenario development approach from a strategic leap control viewpoint is that it can provide insights into how major environmental developments might create new opportunities for refocusing one's strategy. Thus, scenario planning is a way of controlling one's positioning relative to environmental scenario developments. One benefit is that it might, at a relatively early stage, create sensitivity to the opportunities that might arise from such environmental changes.

An interesting note is that the future scenario literature stresses the importance of the learning that comes from active monitoring of events against expectations. This has been succinctly stated in a summary article by Edmunds (1984) in which he conludes:

> Perhaps some would say that it is a waste of time to study the future and its feedback loops so exhaustively. On the other hand, what one knows always becomes clearer by knowing what one does not know.

Much is known about the structure and trend of economic events, commodity flows, resources, population, organizations, industrial, technological, and governmental activities. Much less is known at the macro level about the linkages or feedbacks of the global system, or at the micro-level about changes in individual attitude and values. These changes in micro and macro interactions are the essence of which business strategy and policy is made (i.e., how will people's values shift and what changes environmental interactions may bring). A plausible approach to dealing with these complex interactions is to pursue studies as a mode of examining the probabilities of alternative future scenarios and *then checking which events of scenarios [actually] unfold.* The monitoring of probabilistic alternative futures will improve environmental scanning as a framework for business policy— and at least future studies can help business *strategy process into an enquiring and learning system.* (Edmunds 1984, 45) (emphasis added)

A number of corporations have employed such a scenario development approach for years. Perhaps the most visible of these has been Royal Dutch Shell and the Shell group of companies. In an interesting speech in 1981, P. W. Wack, the then planning director of Shell U.K., reflected on his experience with scenario planning over the previous ten years:

> Thus the fundamental role of the planner is to promote conceptual understanding, rather than provide numerical quantification—though numerical quantification may have an important role to play in the process. Without a sound conceptual framework, the numerical quantifications are virtually meaningless, and it becomes increasingly difficult to sort out which bits of information are relevant to the decision in question.... The basic purpose of scenarios is to provide decision makers with such a framework; it must not only be a practical tool for decision-making, but it must also help to create understanding of those elements of the future which could impinge on the decision.... By allowing plans to be tested against different eventualities, the scenario approach also helps in the development of plans with the greatest degree of resilience.

Jefferson (1981), a Shell economist, has analyzed several dimensions of Shell's experience with the use of scenarios. He delineates the elements, or building blocks, of a typical scenario relevant to the business, each of which has its obvious dimensions for measurement for strategic control:

- macroeconomic growth prospects
- possible political changes and public policy developments
- societal developments affecting corporate objectives and ways of meeting them, individual values and actions

- industry demand prospects (including energy saving, conservation, and increased efficiency in use in Shell's case)
- industry supply prospects
- industry capacity, cost, and price development
- present technology, potential innovations, pace of diffusion, and scope for substitution
- present and prospective competitive environment

Jefferson further comments: "With a high quality scenario team the essential value of its work lies in its qualitative assessments. Thus quantitative assessments should play a subordinate role, being handmaidens to the qualitative assessments by ensuring correspondence with perceived reality. Historical data are usually a help in forming judgments about the future, and are one defence against selective perception and other biases in the exercise of judgment" (1981, 23).

Jefferson also stresses the need to face up to uncertainty and to act constructively in its presence: "Fortunately, Shell's experience with scenario writing since 1971 has been able to offer more than just communication of inherent uncertainty. First, by focussing in a systematic way on the various building blocks it has been impossible to detect a number of 'pre-determined elements' already in the pipeline. While there could be no certainty how these elements would come out at the other end, examination by the scenario team of their likely impact was found to be a great help in increasing awareness of decision makers as to what might happen, and in preparing management for what did happen on many cases" (1981, 26).

Shell's scenario planning, in Jefferson's judgment, was most useful: "All in all, however, the record of a decade of multiple scenario planning in Shell has been a remarkable success. The approach has enabled people to cope much better with uncertainty in a period of unusual turbulence. The scenarios have shed light on a large number of important elements and possible outcomes which have come to pass. Recognition of uncertainty, awareness of some 'pre-determined' elements, and the forewarning of the direction of possible changes have all been achieved" (1981, 31).

Jefferson gave some concrete illustrations of what he saw as the impact of scenario planning at Shell:

> Thus, it has been very noticeable how much lower Shell's growth and demand assumptions were after 1974 in the scenarios than those of competitors, national government, international institutions and forecasting institutes in general. Shell therefore allowed themselves some advance warning on what not to spend money on building or acquir-

ing, and how much might suitably be spent on building or acquiring something else . . . selective strategies were encouraged [but were in fact] geared to weak overall demand . . . these often sombre warnings and indications have not always gone down well or quickly with the more venturesome or traditional spirits geared to the ways of thinking and acting appropriate to the high growth of the 1950's and 1960's. (1981, 35)

Worth noting is that economists tend to think of scenarios as better ways to do more relevant forecasting. For a scenario to be used for strategic management, it must be embedded in a process used and found useful by management. It would then form a robust platform on which to base one's strategic control system. This latter set of issues is addressed implicitly by Wack (1984). He stresses the fact that one of the goals of scenario work is not action but understanding. He concludes that Shell's first phase of their use of scenarios resulted in their having "excellent search tools. These had yet to become effective planning devices" (Wack 1984, 12). As Wack puts it, "although the scenario package had created (among Shell managers) an intellectual interest, its essential failure to be translated into a changed behavior in much of the Shell organization came as a shock and broke through a psychological barrier in our understanding of how to 'design' scenarios geared for decision making" (1984, 24). Wack goes on to point out that unless the decision maker's own mental model of the world is changed, no change in behavior will occur. We return to this topic in the next chapter, where we argue that good strategic control is a powerful force for creating such change.

A significant characteristic of scenarios used in a large organization is the balance they permit between centralization and decentralization. As Wack puts it, "a strategy is the product of a world view; if the world view is changed, widespread decentralized strategic decisions follow without leading to anarchy, more effectively than any centralized planning instructions could bring about." (1984, 30) From their scenario work, they "saw that each nation would be affected so differently by the energy shock that each would have to respond independently. (Shell did in fact decentralize very rapidly, which enabled it to adjust faster to the turbulence it experienced. It is now the most decentralized of major oil companies.)" (1984, 36).

As these extensive quotes from Shell executives clearly indicate, scenario-based strategic control can be an effective approach. We argue that for companies whose planning is based on scenario development, a good strategic control system requires a high degree of qualitative information and hence an unusually well-managed and active process of discussion between relevant experts, planners, and managers. Such a system also needs high-quality experienced staff if it is to function well. This form of strategic control will be largely event driven.

Scenario-based strategic control is not only useful for large corporations; it can be effective in medium-size ones as well. For example, a more recent implementation of scenario control was developed by the CEO and founder of the XYZ Corporation, an $800 million (in 1984) firm, built around a core set of skills in a particular aerospace technology. These skills have been parlayed into consumer and service businesses as they have expanded their original market in the high-technology business. As their original core became larger and potentially ran the risk of plateauing, they faced the question of how to grow profitably. They decided that the most critical component of their strategy and the one that would benefit from being dealt with via a formal process was that of understanding those aspects of the external environment that were undergoing major change and their implications for the internal strengths and weaknesses of the organization.

The CEO decided that everyone in senior management had the potential to contribute to the "lateral" thinking that was required. He initially established five steps, which themselves were the subject of suggestions and debate. The steps that were proposed to the management team by the CEO were as follows:

1. Define the premises. We have always been affected by demographic, economic, environmental, geopolitical, and technological change. The pace of that change is accelerating, and the task of this phase is to anticipate the winds of change—to define and test the premises that will shape the future.

2. Determine the business potentials associated with the premises.

3. Perform business analysis. Industries and opportunities highlighted in Phase 2 would be profiled, and a business analysis would define the players, their size, and concentration. What is the size related to risk, the downside dangers versus potential bounty? What do we bring in value-added to ensure a niche not easily open to others?

4. Determine fit with our company. This phase will balance all the collected premises, potential, and financial findings on industries and specific companies against our objectives. Given the results of this, do we want to do it, would this new business provide the right fit and balance for us?

5. Initiate executive actions. In this phase, executive action takes over to decide the approach to execution. Included are the people chemistry, establishing benchmarks, and potential policies.

A process involving outside experts and management in varying combinations was then established. The key output was to reach consensus on the "driving assumptions," the most critical assertions, which were then to be rediscussed periodically as events changed or time milestones were reached. This approach rests on the (in our view, valid) assumption that intelligent "sensitized" managers will intuitively pick up signals from the environment, which can be made explicit and acted on if managers are given a chance to step back from the pressures of ongoing work to collate and prioritize such signals, and from that learning process, managers will define the changes in course that ought to be made.

This whole process assumes that the organization is being run effectively—that is, that the policies and procedures for ongoing internal operations are appropriate. Without such a stable base, one cannot realistically generate powerful scenario planning, because the key people may well be distracted by intense firefighting. The development of realistic scenarios is a highly time- and energy-consuming process, particularly for the key managers who must be heavily involved and mentally committed. Only in situations in which the corporation feels a particular wartime urgency to sensibly reexamine its long-term positions in the environment can one expect that the organization will spend time on such scenario efforts.

The question of cultural fit should also be considered. Scenario planning and control works best when a wide cross section of the organization participates openly. This implies trust and a willingness to expose oneself and one's ideas—aspects that are not present in all organizations. In their absence, scenario planning and the related strategic control will be difficult to use effectively.

These methods of strategic thinking represent the four approaches we have found in use in today's corporations that are specifically addressed to wartime conditions. As such, they are different from classical strategic planning. As indicated, they have major implications for strategic control—implications found most effective by the organizations using these techniques.

We turn now to the question that inevitably arises from the fact that no organization operates indefinitely in either peacetime or wartime conditions: What are the indications for changing one's strategic control approach from one to the other?

WHEN TO MOVE FROM MOMENTUM TO LEAP STRATEGIC CONTROL

Strategic momentum control activities are carried out on an ongoing basis and provide management with routine scanning signals regarding how one's strategies are evolving. These signals will be a major source of inputs for the decision to shift from a peacetime strategic control mode to a wartime one. Typically, this decision will be made by top management on the basis of a multitude of signals, which in total provide a phenomenological pattern indicating the necessity for change. Typically, signals may come from the following sources:

1. The annual planning process can reveal that the basic underlying assumptions on which plans were based no longer are realistic. For the United States car industry, for instance, the changing costs of energy led to a fundamental rethinking of the industry's basic strategy regarding model size and mix.

2. Through incremental strategic control, it may become apparent that critical environmental assumptions may be shifting. For instance, one's pricing strategy may have to change when one learns that a competitor is building up additional capacity. Thus, the firm must find ways to meet this intensified competitive climate. Another example would be a major shift in customers' attitudes toward one's product, which may call for a dramatic response. The signal to shift to a wartime mode of strategic control may also be associated with a drop in bottom-line performance. Changes in key environmental factors are particularly important if incremental strategic control is to provide sufficient sensitizing and early warning signals.

3. Testing of one's own strategies relative to what generically should be the expected normal case may also lead to warning signals. Environmental circumstances may render one's strategy more and more counterintuitive, but such developments can be overlooked in the absence of testing.

4. The functioning of administrative systems can also provide signals that peacetime conditions may be changing. This situation can manifest itself in an increasing number of dysfunctional actions and internal friction associated with these administrative systems. More and more of the organization's energy can be spent on internal bickering and quarreling rather than on spending the effort necessary to adjust to the environment. Taken together with signals of other sorts, this can be a reliable indication that extensive strategic realignment may be warranted.

Top management must be alert for signals indicating the need for a shift from peacetime to wartime approaches. Thus, a prerequisite is that both top management and its team avoid becoming complacent. One reason why complacency sets in is that peacetime strategic control typically portrays a picture of things going reasonably well; this sense of success can in itself foster maintenance of the status quo. This situation can be further magnified by the fact that top management in many organizational cultures tend to receive potentially troublesome signals only after considerable delays, and they are then often "packaged" in considerable "cotton." Positive signals may be reported out of context or with the ommission of important qualifications, again disguising potential negative nuances. These types of biases make it even harder for top management to foster the necessary problem orientation and a culture of readiness to deal with major discontinuities early. If a problem is not recognized, due to bias and complacency, a serious delay in responding to a wartime situation may result.

A necessary approach, therefore, is for top management to build confidence in its contemplated actions through examining the signals that it receives and through different syntheses of this information. This might include hands-on discussions with executives at lower levels in the organization and with critical sources of information in the environment, such as key customers. Also, it might include a careful review of the initial ameliorating actions that have typically been taken. This in-depth probing can lead top management to conclude that a peacetime approach is insufficient for achieving the desired results.

In the final analysis, the performance of a top management team is determined by whether the team is able to make good calls in shifting from peacetime to wartime conditions. We stress that this decision is for top management. The line management organization further down in the organizational structure would normally continue to pursue the sorting out of problems through peacetime means until challenged by top management to adjust.

Let us briefly discuss a final dimension of moving from momentum control to leap control relating to the atitude of strategic planners and controllers. These staff executives can become closely attached to the management systems and processes that they have either developed or been appointed to manage. Naturally, they believe in these systems; if not, they would not have these staff jobs. They may have difficulty admitting that more dramatic ameliorating actions might be needed for certain situations than simply sorting them out through peacetime processes. Thus, one might expect that such staff executives might actually fight or resist a move toward significantly changed conditions. A particularly unfortunate side effect of this situation is that these valuable staff executives thereby might operate less efficiently during such a strategic leap control phase. Good strategic planners and controllers should be comfortable with change and acknowledge the need for peacetime and wartime approaches depending on circumstances. If staff executives have come to believe that the power of either the momentum control systems or the leap control systems with which they are associated is so strong that no changes are warranted at any time, then such managers possess a serious weakness.

Such a situation recently arose in the large and diversified U.S. manufacturing company described next. We believe that this story will appear familiar to many managers, for the situation is not uncommon even among well-managed and high-performing firms such as this one.

This several billion dollar corporation had installed strategic planning for the first time in the mid-1970s to improve the organization's response to a (generally) changing external environment. The first year, they hired a strategic planning consulting firm, which did an effective job of teaching senior management and screening applicants to identify a possible full-time planner to be hired by the organization. They succeeded in attracting an MBA who had had three years of experience as a member of another major corporation's planning staff. He came in with energy, built a planning system that helped to clarify a number of issues facing the corporation, and worked with the management to help them make some tough decisions about incremental redirection.

This planner then went on to install and institutionalize a planning process. However, after awhile, the CEO and other senior executives began to make major decisions outside the system; they would not use the formal planning system installed by the planner. This upset the planner, and he spent a great deal of time and effort haranguing senior management about the need to use what he believed was an effective system. What he did not understand was that conditions in the external environment had changed again, and now it was "war." That is, the organization was moving into a period of discontinuity in its marketplaces, and as such, the systems built for peacetime use were no longer appropriate. Senior executives were making choices based on facts plus their experiences, and the choices they were making would transform the organization. Only extrapolative, incremental decisions could be made as a result of the data collected by the planning process. Such incremental decisions would merely lead to modification of business as usual. Given the changed organizational environment, key executives clearly knew that incremental modifications would not create value for their stakeholders.

Not understanding the reasons for the executives not using his planning system, the planner became more and more frustrated and finally left the organization. He believed that management was unsympathetic and unsupportive of him and his planning efforts. However, what was occurring was a basic shift in the type of planning required and therefore the type of strategic control required if the organization was to be effective. Monitoring actual performance against the plan did not provide the kind of inputs necessary to reshape the direction of the corporation. Strategic leap control must take into account discontinuities in the environment; it is insufficient to monitor performance against plan. This fundamental failure on the part of the planner and the chief executive to recognize what was happening was unfortunate but is all too often typical of organizational response to change.

FROM STRATEGIC LEAP CONTROL TO STRATEGIC MOMENTUM CONTROL

With appropriate strategic control in a wartime situation, the organization will achieve a "win"—that is, a broad understanding of its new strategic options. The clarification of these options must be accompanied by a growing sense of confidence among mangement that the identified strategic options can be pulled off, given the resources that the organization possesses. The end of a need for strategic leap control has been reached when an organizational convergence exists toward committing new strategic direction for the firm.

If such a convergence does not take place, then wartime conditions are still in effect. The organization must keep on searching for strategic directions via strategic leap control means until, in principle, no more resources are left in the company. Properly executed, such approaches should lead to positive outcome before such a dramatic state is reached.

When the conditions for new peacetime settings are reached, the organization must determine how to implement the new strategic direction. Further fleshing out of strategic objectives accompanied by a delineation of strategic implementation programs are typically needed. It is important that the organization approaches these issues by using conventional momentum control means (i.e., strategic planning, strategic control, revamped administrative systems). The settling into a new peacetime period does not imply that the energy of the organization should be slowed down. On the contrary, the energy of the organization must be focused and channeled into an administrative systems momentum mode so as to continue to achieve maximum effects from the energies generated. This shift in energy from a wartime mode toward more systemic uses is therefore critical.

A potential problem in making this shift might be that the organization is so "psyched out" that it might find it hard to settle into the different disciplines of momentum control. In addition, the shift may be delayed by the belief that momentum control is still irrelevant. A false sense of achievement is sometimes generated by continuing all the action that takes place in a wartime setting; the problem is that this activity may produce a good deal of smoke but little value-added. Also, the planning and control staff is typically in a relatively weak position to facilitate the shift from wartime to peacetime control if their resistance prevented them from playing an important role in moving from peacetime to wartime control. The organization might perceive these staff executives as being out of touch or having relatively little credibility.

Again, top management must insist on and facilitate the changing of gear from wartime to peacetime control. This can be done in three ways:

1. Clear, explicit statements that the organization must return to the systematic treatment of planning and control to pull off the new strategic options to which it has committed itself.

2. Promoting the peacetime discipline through one's own actions. Top management must avoid taking impulsive steps that may make sense on their own but which may give conflicting role model signals to the organization. In periods of shifting to peacetime conditions, it is particularly important that top management pay close attention to making use of the planning and control systems and that they exercise the necessary discipline and restrain themselves.

3. Appointment of new staff planners and controllers if a belief exists that the present planners and controllers have lost their credibility. Strategic controllers who adapted to wartime conditions and retained their organizational clout would be valuable organizational members.

AN OVERALL VIEW OF STRATEGY AND STRATEGIC CONTROL

In Chapter 4, we discussed the methods of strategic control as they arise from the classical or peacetime models of strategic planning. In this section, we reviewed some of the more recent approaches to strategic planning and their control implications. These discussions have been based on our premise that the strategic control system of a firm must be matched to its strategic planning process. However, that leaves us with an unanswered question: Given our assertions about environmental discontinuities, what should a firm do to maintain its long-term viability? We have positioned strategic control as the process of sensitizing a firm to impending changes and as a mechanism for coping with such changes. The learning that comes from a comparison of "where we are" with "where we wanted to be" provides the base on which to build action programs. These programs under conditions of momentum control will inevitably be different from those appropriate for recalibrating the direction and size of a strategic leap into new products or markets. Presumably, as McGraw-Hill began to sense the shift from the magazine publishing business to the information dissemination business, they began to rethink what strategic moves might be appropriate. Assessing the implications of new technology and the low-level preliminary moves of new players such as Citibank would have been typical moves in a wartime strategic control setting. This clearly differs from monitoring this quarter's or this year's bottom-line profit performance as the primary indicators. In periods of discontinuity, by the time the peacetime indicators register a change, it may well be too late; the market opportunity could be gone.

Matching the strategic control system to leverage the effort devoted in the organization to strategy fromulation and implementation is a sensible way to proceed. However, it should not be forgotten that occasionally the whole approach to strategy should change. Being sensitive to this larger readjustment is crucial and not always done.

At the most aggregate level this involves moving from the set of "momentum control" thinking and techniques we outlined in Chapter 4 to those appropriate for "leap control". Such change does not stop at the aggregate level as the kind of learning we are describing results in continuing change within our two broad categories. For example, one major oil company has moved from a primary emphasis on a scenario approach to strategic planning and control to one that gives greatly increased emphasis on strategic field analysis. This movement between approaches is a natural outgrowth of the shifting demands in the external world coupled with the learning that takes place with the executives. Good strategic control has an enormous influence on that learning.

One further lever is available to the organization. This lever is the constructive use of information technology as the engine to drive the strategic control process both when momentum control or when leap control is appropriate. Information technology is useful in its own right—a subject we turn to in the next chapter. However, it also provides the excuse to rethink how we ought to search certain conclusions and the information that would be most appropriate. For both reasons, the careful use of the new technologies is important and enables the successful use of strategic control.

6

Strategic Control and Diversification: Managing Scope and Consistency

HIERARCHIES OF STRATEGIC CONTROL

Just as there are hierarchies of strategics (Hofer and Schendel 1978), there are also hierarchies of strategic control. At the corporate level, strategic control usually focuses on maintaining a balance among the various business activities of the corporation as a whole. At the business level, which typically coincides with the divisional level, strategic control is principally concerned with maintaining the competitive position of the firm in a particular industry or business. Finally, at the functional level, the role of strategic control becomes one of developing and enhancing function-based distinctive competences.

However, although the concept of strategic control remains valid at all three levels, its scope and significance increase as we move up the hierarchy (see Figure 6.1). At the functional level, operational control assumes relatively greater significance, since maximizing resource productivity is usually the primary strategic concern at this level. At the business level, the role of operational control becomes less, while that of strategic control increases. Being sensitive to shifting technologies, to evolving industry and market structures, and to changing needs for interactions among internal value-creating activities are among the key strategic control activities at this level. Finally, at the corporate level, strategic control assumes even greater significance. Exploiting economies of scope inherent in the product-market diversity of the firm, operationalizing potentials for synergy, and ongoing redeployment of the firm's critical resources to match changing opportunities and threats become the primary objectives of strategic control at this level.

Figure 6.1   Relative Importance of Different Categories of Control at Different Levels of Organizational Hierarchy

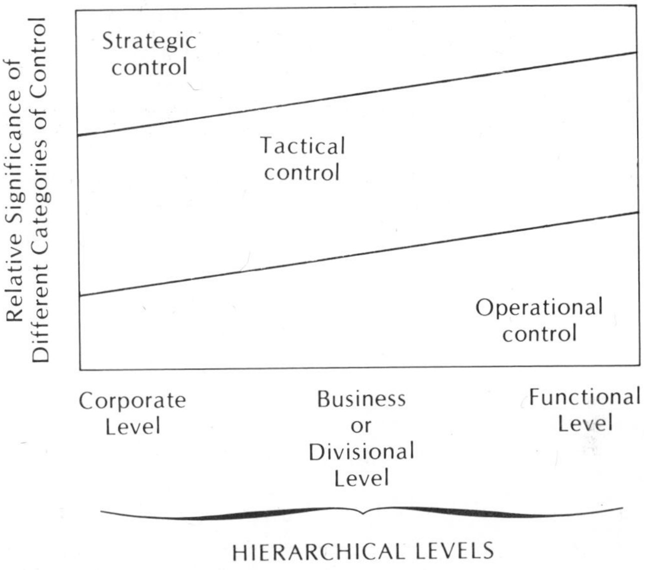

Thus, at each hierarchical level there are different elements that need to be monitored and evaluated as part of the strategic control system.

STRATEGIC CONTROL IN DIFFERENT TYPES OF COMPANIES

In much of the strategic management literature, small companies, particularly those that are privately held, and not-for-profit organizations are excluded from practical consideration. This seems perfectly justifiable to us when one is talking about formalizing and institutionalizing many of the sophisticated management systems for planning and control. Small organizations have totally different information needs; one person, for example, can frequently readily comprehend all that is going on in the various functions or with principal competitors. Although the formalization of these activities with their forms and staffs may not be appropriate for small organizations, the need for planning and control is, however, very much there. Indeed, one can make the point that planning and control become more necessary, as the small organization has neither the size to absorb fluctuations nor the slack resources to turn loose to fix a particular problem. With a small organization, one or two key players must perform these strategic functions informally, relying on their personal time and efforts to make them successful. Although informal, they can nonetheless be real, and informality can benefit from prior understanding of frameworks and concepts.

Similarly, even among large companies, the nature and extent of strategic control, particularly at the corporate level, may vary depending on the extent of diversification. As mentioned earlier, strategic control at the corporate level is critically concerned with exploiting synergy and scope benefits, the potentials for both of which increase with diversification. This is partiacularly true in the case of related diversification but, as we shall argue, is also at least partially true even for unrelated diversification.

In this chapter, we present some perspectives on strategic control at the corporate level in diversified firms. However, this does not mean that the concept of strategic control is applicable only at this level and in such firms. We believe that the fundamental concept of strategic control is applicable to all types of companies and to all the three hierarchical levels discussed earlier. However, we wish to make an analytical distinction between the strategic control issues that are general and applicable to all firms and those that specifically arise in the context of managing diversification. In any diversified firm, both these components of strategic control are applicable, even at the corporate level. The preceeding chapters have dealt with the operational issues of strategic control in general. However, we believe that the diversification phenomenon per se raises some unique and interesting issues with regard to strategic control. Our objective in this chapter is to provide a conceptual framework for understanding these issues.

THE DIVERSIFICATION PHENOMENON

Many reasons have been suggested to explain the diversification phenomenon in U.S. corporations, including stability-risk diversification, portfolio balancing based on the generation and need for cash resources, exploiting market power, strategic access to critical resources and distribution channels, utilizing spare resources such as managerial talent and entrepreneurship, escape from sunset industries, and empire building by ambitious managers (see Wells 1984 for a comprehensive review). However, a number of researchers (Rumelt 1974; Salter and Weinhold 1979) have documented the fact that diversification without the benefit of some form of synergy carries no economic benefit for the firm or its shareholders. We therefore start from the premise that the survival of a diversified firm depends on the existence and exploitation of some synergy. Such synergies arise from the scope of the firm's operations: from the potential of sharing resources across its many activities. These scope economies provide the strategic rationale for diversification, and thus the monitoring and nurturing of these economies give rise to the special concerns of strategic control in the context of the diversification phenomenon.

ECONOMIES OF SCOPE AND SYNERGY

In economic theory, economies of scope are seen as arising from the "sub-additivity" of different production functions (Baumol, Panzer, and Willig 1982) (i.e., when the cost of joint production of two products is less than the cost of producing them separately). Such cost reduction takes place, for example, when one or more of the inputs to the production process have "public goods" characteristics. The economies arise because such goods (such as technical knowledge), once acquired for use in producing one item, are available at zero cost for use in the production of others.

However, a relatively broader definition of scope arises from a literal and intuitive understanding of the term. A company may operate in many markets and deal in many products. Such diversity in the scope of its operations creates certain potentials for sharing resources, thereby increasing the overall efficiency of resource utilization. Such resources may be tangible, such as cash, equipments, patents, or brand names, or intangible, such as corporate culture, organizational skills, or learning abilities. The sharing may take place across functions, products, or markets. A key component of strategic control in diversified firms is to obtain the greatest possible benefits from exploiting the economies that may arise from the scope of the firm's operations.

Figure 6.2 presents a framework for analyzing the sources and applications of scope economies in diversified firms. The principal sources of scope economies and the related strategic control points are three: shared assets, shared external relations, and shared learning. The framework suggests some examples of how each of these sources can generate benefits in cases of both product and market diversifications. The sources and some of the examples are briefly explained next.

Figure 6.2 Scope Economies in Product and Market Diversification

SOURCES OF SCOPE ECONOMIES	Product Diversification	Market Diversification
Shared Assets	Factory automation with flexibility to produce multiple products. (Ford in Brazil)	Global brand name (Coca-Cola)
Shared External Relations	Using common distribution channel for multiple products (Matsushita in Japan)	Servicing multinational customers worldwide (Citibank)
Shared Learning	Sharing R&D in computer and communications businesses (NEC)	Pooling knowledge developed in different markets (Procter and Gamble for liquid Tide)

Sources of Scope Economies

Shared Assets. Shared physical assets can be cash, equipment, brand names, and so on. The case of sharing cash across different businesses is an old concept and lies at the heart of the portfolio strategies popularized by the Boston Consulting Group and others (see Hax and Majluf 1984 for a critical review of different portfolio models). While the BCG model has been criticized both for a vulgar vocabulary (Andrews 1981) and for oversimplification (*Fortune* 1981), the underlying concept of building up attractive new businesses by using the surplus generated by other mature businesses is both robust and widely practiced.

One of the key advantages of factory automation using robots is the enhanced ability to share such equipment across different products or activities. Progress in flexible manufacturing systems suggests that the day may not be far when a factory can be switched from one product to a totally different product, merely by replacing preprogrammed cassettes in centralized control equipments. One of the effects of such systems would be to expand the benefits of scope available to multiproduct firms.

Let us discuss the strategic control implication of such flexibility with reference to a specific example. A major multinational automobile manufacturer incurred 30 percent additional capital costs so as to build into its plant in a high-inflation developing country the flexibility either to produce complete automobiles for the local market or to manufacture specific components on a global scale for feeding other manufacturing plants of the company. This considerably enhanced the company's ability to respond flexibly to changes in the local environment. When the economy ran in high gear, inflation was high, as was the local demand for cars, and the company switched fully to asssembling complete automobiles to supply the local market. Periodically, as the government took drastic belt-tightening actions to control inflation and foreign debt, the demand for cars slumped, but the connected movement in exchange rates made the plant attractive as a low-cost source of components to the global manufacturing system of the company. A lot of other flexibilities had to be built into the overall system so that the company could exercise such options, but clearly it substantially enhanced its strategic control capabilities by deliberately creating such flexibilities.

Developing global brand names is another example of how a firm can benefit from sharing an asset across products or functions. In the case of Coca-Cola, most of the value-adding activities are carried out by independent local bottlers. Yet, it is a global business that is largely based on exploiting a brand name globally.

Shared External Relations. A second important source of economy of scope is shared external relations: with customers, suppliers, distributors, governments, and other institutions.

One major driving force that made many firms multinational was following their customers across the globe (Terpstra 1982). Thus, banks followed their clients abroad, just as manufacturers of automobile components followed the automobile companies. In another variation, trading companies, for over two hundred years, have expanded into new businesses to meet different requirements of existing customers.

The fundamental source of Matsushita's advantage over Sony in the global consumer electronics market arises from its superior strategic position within Japan. Relationship with distributors is a critical component of this strategic advantage. Distribution of consumer electronics products in Japan is mostly carried out by franchised retailers of the different manufacturers, who maintain close relations with the principals and carry only their products. The system depends on the manufacturers producing and supplying every type of consumer electronics and household appliance so that the retailer can obtain the benefits of scale and thereby become viable. Matsushita and Toshiba have succeeded in building up far more extensive distribution systems than, say, Sony or Sanyo, primarily because they are full-line producers of consumer durables, while the others are not. This is an example of benefits of scope across products that arise from sharing a common distribution channel.

Let us briefly consider the strategic control implications of this situation, particularly from the perspective of Matsushita. The distribution channel is clearly one of its major strategic strengths. The company must therefore continuously monitor the sources of this strength and revitalize it so as to maintain the competitive advantage. It must monitor the buying patterns of customers and guard against a gradual switch to another channel as social and demographic structures change. If such alternative channels emerge, the company must understand the implications and must be ready to defend its position, either by preempting that channel or by building up its own strengths in that channel. It must also constantly review the continued appropriateness of the locations, designs, and marketing strategies of its existing resellers and modify them to match changing social patterns. It must also guard against overloading the existing channel (i.e., maintain the golden balance between providing a sufficiently large number of items for the resellers to obtain their own scale and scope benefits and providing too many items, leading to some receiving inadequate attention or promotion). The consequences of failing to maintain such strategic control over a key success factor is manifest from the well-known case of the Swiss watchmakers. They ignored the gradual shift from specialty jewelers to department stores as the principal channel for selling watches and, in the course of one decade, lost their worldwide market leadership that had taken a century to build.

Shared Knowledge. Even a casual visitor to Japan's NEC cannot escape the slogan of "C and C": computers and communication. The fundamental belief of the firm is that its even strengths in both of these merging technologies is its greatest strategic asset. IBM and Fujitsu are computer companies; Ericsson, AT&T, and Hitachi are communication companies. NEC believes that as the two technologies merge, its deep knowledge of both will provide scope advantages that will give it a competitive edge over all the companies who have technological strength in only one of the two fields. Both Philips and Siemens have voiced the same view. The technological collaborations between Ericsson and Honeywell, and between AT&T and Philips, and the acquisition of Rolm by IBM provide evidence that many giants in both the fields see the need for building similar scope benefits in their own organizations.

This is an example of how strategic advantages may arise from sharing knowledge across different products or industries. Similarly, integrating knowledge and learning acquired in different locations can also provide sources of scope advantage. Consider the following example:

> When Procter & Gamble Co. introduced a product called Tide back in 1946, American technology was at work. P&G researchers had found chemicals that get clothes cleaner, even in hard water, and because of their resourcefulness, the first successful synthetic detergent was born.
>
> P&G recently introduced its new Liquid Tide, but the product has a distinctly international heritage. A new ingredient that helps suspend dirt in wash water came from the company's research center near P&G's Cincinnati headquarters. But the formula for Liquid Tide's surfactants, or cleaning agents, was developed by P&G agents in Japan. The ingredients that fight the mineral salts present in hard water come from P&G's scientists in Brussels. "We drew on ideas and technology from around the world," says John Leikhim, who headed the product development team. (*Wall Street Journal*, 29 April 1985)

Sources of Synergy

Such a combination of technologies and ideas was possible only because of P&G's multinational scope of operations. Liquid Tide is perhaps a dramatic example of exploiting market scope by sharing and integrating knowledge developed in different markets.

In an alternative but closely related conceptualization, Wells (1984) has suggested a typology of synergies that leads to creation of value through diversification. His conceptual structure neatly captures the dimensions along which diversified organizations must begin to think about building their strategic control system. In the following paragraphs, we briefly describe the different sources of synergy suggested by this typology. It is not implied that any one firm should care about all these sources at all points of time. What is important is that the diversified organization must consciously think through and identify the particular aspects of synergy that are most crucial at a given moment, and its strategic control system must focus on those dimensions.

The three categories of synergy proposed by Wells are as follows:

Shared Operations. Synergy can be found in shared operations such as R&D, marketing, and procurement. Scale economies in common parts of the value chains in the firm's different businesses may provide a source for creating value in excess of the associated costs of increased coordination, possible lack of accountability, and the ambiguity inherent in managing shared resources. Thus, a common sales force or distribution channel can be used to sell two products, basic research in a common field can be applied to develop new products in different industries, and a manufacturing plant may produce components for both digital watches and pocket calculators. In other words, this form of synergy can arise from sharing physical assets or external relations (or both) developed by the firm.

Distinctive Competence. Distinctive competence is the ability of the firm to perform effectively in certain contexts or knowledge domains. Often, such context-specific skills are embedded in the individuals the firm employs and in the way they are organized to achieve a common purpose. Distinctive competence may lie in special entrepreneurial, managerial, or technical skills that a firm may possess (e.g., managing high-growth industries, ability to survive in oligopolistic or regulated environments, or marketing leisure products).

While running the risk of oversimplification, we suggest that the automobile industry is a good example of how distinctive competence may differ among firms operating in the same industry. The argument can be made that high cost-efficiency and product quality in large-scale centralized manufacturing are two of the principal sources of competitive advantage on which Toyota has built up its worldwide position in the passenger car market. Ford, on the other hand, has traditionally attempted to build its strength by combining a strong coordination mechanism with global dispersion of its value-added so as to exploit factor-cost economies and also to overcome regulatory barriers. Finally, Fiat has usually positioned itself at the other extreme, developing a distinctive competence in dealing with national governments so as to obtain protection from these more efficient global competitors in exchange for setting up largely self-sufficient local operations (see Bartlett 1984 17–18).

Shared Image and Values. The image of a firm, for instance of high product quality (e.g., Procter and Gamble), may be so strong as to be transferable to a new domain (such as paper tissues). Such synergy is created by maintaining a common purpose and a set of common values across a product or market portfolio.

Each of these sources of synergy, however is not static but dynamic, and as such the strategic control system is even more necessary. The sources change due to changes both within the firm and in its environment. Thus, a quality image based on a flagship product may erode as the core product falls out of step with rapid tecnological advances. Similarly, a new business entered on the assumption of a particularly strong distinctive competence (say, R&D for

Hewlett-Packard) may flounder as the required key competence changes (from technology to marketing, as in the personal computer business), or a conglomerate built on an exceptional pool of entrepreneurial or managerial talent may lose its strategic advantage as those individuals resign or retire.

Thus, diversified firms need a process of continuous monitoring to check for continued validity of the synergies that justified their diversification and for the possibility that new synergy potentials may have been created in the process of continuing environmental and organizational changes. Such monitoring forms a key aspect of strategic control in large and diversified companies.

STRATEGIC CONSISTENCY: INTERNAL AND EXTERNAL

Scope benefits are the positive aspects of diversification arising from the commonness across products and markets that creates the potential for sharing and synergy. However, each of the components in a diversified firm also possesses certain uniqueness creating differences in the way they should be managed. Internalizing these differences creates costs of coordination and control, which constitute the negative side of diversification. Strategic control in such firms must be concerned with monitoring not only the benefits but also the costs of exploiting synergies.

Consider a firm such as N. V. Philips, the global electronics giant. It manufactures products as traditional as electric light bulbs and as sophisticated as defense-related radar and guidance-control equipments. It is a global player in industries such as consumer electronics, telecommunication switching and terminal equipments, computers, medical systems, IC chips, and small domestic appliances. Some of these products are highly research intensive; others are considerably less so. In the terminology of Porter (1985), some of the industries are global, offering significant advantages from worldwide integration and coordination of activities, while some others are multidomestic, offering rich benefits of differentiation, decentralization, and local autonomy at the level of country subsidiaries.

The company faces a similar degree of diversity in the markets in which it operates. They vary by size, local competitive intensity, extent of regulation, customer tastes and preferences, and administrative histories of the subsidiaries. Given these differences in the local environment, the company would have a difficult time managing all of them on the same basis and through common systems and processes. Some, such as the subsidiary in the United States, may need to be given significant autonomy for business, historical, or legal reasons. Others, such as the country operations in India or Brazil, may have to be treated as virtually stand-alone units due to regulatory considerations. A world-scale manufacturing subsidiary in Taiwan or Singapore may, for coordination purposes, need to be managed with a high degree of centralization. The European subsidiaries, in contrast, may have to be strongly interlinked among themselves precisely for exploiting scope economies.

Given this diversity of strategic needs and demands of different subunits, the company can pursue a broad range of alternatives in terms of the strategic consistency among them. At one extreme, the differences can be ignored, to the extent possible, and the company may seek *internal* strategic and administrative consistency. Such internal consistency can create benefits of standardization and efficiency in implementation. At the other extreme, the firm may seek *external* consistency between each subunit and its relevant environment, managing each operation differently with tailor-made strategies and administrative systems. While such an approach may lead to better external fits, it also results in increasing internal inconsistencies and in ambiguities, and can lead to a chaotic state. The costs of coordination can increase dramatically, and control may become almost infeasible. This is a dilemma that every diversified firm faces to varying extents depending on the homogeneity of its product-market portfolio. In a holding company such as those classified by Rumelt (1974) as unrelated-diversified or conglomerate, the costs of seeking internal strategic consistency may be too high, and the company may follow a strategy of external consistency for each business. In such a situation, corporate-level strategic control reduces primarily to issues of portfolio management. For a company that is diversified in highly related businesses, the trade-off between internal and external consistency becomes much more delicate and subtle, requiring more fine-grained analysis of the costs and benefits of both.

BALANCING INTERNAL AND EXTERNAL CONSISTENCIES: THE ROLE OF STRATEGIC CONTROL

One major purpose of strategic control in diversified organizations is to continually reevaluate the costs and benefits of internal and external consistencies so that the firm might obtain the optimum balance between the two. This optimum point depends as much on the state of the external environment facing each of the different businesses, markets, or activities as it does on the organizational and managerial histories and competencies of the organization.

Coca-Cola presents an interesting example to illustrate this issue in the context of geographic diversification.[1] Some of the functions involved in producing and marketing "the real thing" all over the world are intensely local in scope; bottling and distribution are prime examples. Some others, such as creating and maintaining brand image and recognition or designing efficient bottling plants, are essentially global in scope. Carrying out both these sets of functions in-house would clearly lead to internalizing enormous differences within the company with regard to organizing, coordinating, and control systems. Instead of creating such internal inconsistencies, Coca-Cola has decided to externalize those functions that are purely local in scope and carry out in-house only those activities that can be integrated and managed globally. Such selective externalization is one way to maintain external consistency without creating excessive inconsistencies within the firm.

Another example of externalizing to avoid diseconomies of internal inconsistencies is IBM's decision to set up a distinct and almost stand-alone organization to handle the personal computer business. The strategic needs to succeed in the PC market were believed to be so different from IBM's traditional strengths in the mainframe business that a separate organizational system was required to avoid the ambiguities and conflicts that would arise if the business was handled within the existing management structure.

An example of failing to recognize the problems of internal inconsistency is that of EMI's unsuccessful venture into the CT scanner business (EMI and the CT Scanner 1983). Despite having innovated the technology and having built up an almost overwhelming market lead by 1977, the company started losing money in this business from mid–1979, succumbed to a takeover bid from Thorn Electric Industries, and divested the business by 1980.

To a large extent, EMI's failure was due to its inability to deal with the enormous difference between the new CT scanner business and its traditional businesses in the music, electronics, and leisure industries. It was a highly U.K.-centered company, while the principal market for CT scanners was in the United States. The top management of the company could not cope with the vastly different strategic demands brought about by the diversification into the medical equipment field, and the growing internal inconsistencies, in the absence of adequate organizational capabilities for dealing with them, led to the ultimate failure of the company.

Let us briefly recapitulate the central thrust of our argument. In

---

1. This example was suggested to us by Donald Lessard, professor of international management at MIT.

this chapter, we have suggested that monitoring and exploiting the potential for synergy is a special objective of strategic control in diversified organizations. We have discussed the sources and benefits of synergy in the context of a number of specific examples and have suggested the role of strategic control in operationalizing the relevant economies. However, synergy is not without cost. First, it creates the need for additional coordination, which has its own costs. Further, and more relevant at the strategic level, attempts to obtain the benefits of synergy may lead to inappropriate enforcing of strategic commonness among businesses. We have framed the issue in terms of internal and external strategic consistencies and have argued that a primary objective of strategic control is to maintain a balance between these two.

An excessive focus on synergies may lead to a loss of responsiveness in individual businesses, while minute adjustment of each operation to achieve a perfect fit with its own environment may lead to loss of scope economies and, in the extreme, can lead to an internal diversity that can overwhelm the company. An effective and ongoing strategic control system can identify either of these two excesses and can provide to corporate-level managers the early warning signals required for taking remedial actions.

7

Operationalizing Strategic Control

INTRODUCTION

In this chapter we discuss several issues central to operationalizing strategic control. We shall focus on the roles of certain key executives in implementing the strategic control process. This includes the role of various eclectic management teams, above all the roles of top management—a central theme of this chapter. Also, the chapter deals with the controller in the strategic control system and suggests that this individual's key function is to serve as a change agent, catalyst, and custodian of the strategic process, safeguarding against the degeneration of strategic control over time. The question of managing the evolution of the strategic control processes over time is also discussed. These issues normally apply equally to situations of momentum control and leap control, except when specifically noted otherwise.

The strategic control process can easily become overly bureaucratic and stale over time. Managerial liveliness and creativity can be driven out, and routinized, noncreative efforts can become more and more prevalent. This can manifest itself in several ways. The emphasis on critical environmental factors may erode. Gradually, the strategic control process may become more and more internal, more and more focused on familiar paths. Thus, one may end up discussing old themes over and over again, while evolving new environmental issues will not be sufficiently emphasized. Often, not enough discussion may take place about which key executives should at any time be involved in critical areas of strategic control, in what ways, and how they are expected to contribute. Rather, the process may become bureaucratized, staff oriented, and delegated in an undiscriminating way; the line may become more and more passive and peripheral to the process. Too many forms, too much passing around of reports, and too little face-to-face interaction among key managers is a trademark of stale strategic control.

Prior characteristics such as these should be warning signals that the strategic control process is starting to degenerate. What are some approaches to stem such tendencies toward degeneration? Stated differently, how can organizations continue to maintain considerable commitment toward meaningful and creative strategic control efforts? We give four recommendations for maintaining creativity in strategic control as the process evolves over time. The first is making extensive use of creative teams, sets of executives drawn together from different parts of the organization, not necessarily always following the formal organizational structure of the company. Second, top management must be directly involved in the sensitizing process, maintaining control on the way key success factors are monitored. Third, strategic control must focus on the key bottlenecks among the critical success factors as well as on changes in the factors themselves. What may be impeding the critical success factors, and how can the strategic control process be more issue driven in terms of focusing on these critical phenomena? Finally, the strategic control process must be managed so that budgets, formats, agendas, and so on are tailor-made and flexible to meet the demands of the particular strategic context at hand. Let us discuss each of these four issues in more detail.

Strategic Control Teams

Strategic control teams should be formed when particularly complex, important, or sensitive environmental factors (or a combination of these) need to be scanned and understood. Such teams should be formed by bringing together a cross-disciplinary set of managers. It is desirable that these managers have different backgrounds and different experiences. Even though these teams should typically be line manager-dominated, to emphasize the decision-making implications of particular environmental factors under review, selected staff specialists might also participate, which will normally help in analysis and interpretation. Further, the strategic control teams may have both senior and junior people involved, thus drawing on the talents of the entire organization without being overly constrained by the formal, hierarchical organizational structure positioning of each particular executive. An interesting note is that such teams are commonly used in Japanese organizations (Pascale and Athos 1981).

The strategic control team structure overlays the operating structure. When critical environmental factors emerge, the line manager in charge of a particular strategy can get help from a team of powerful executives following the line manager's particular strategy. Each manager responsible for a difficult strategy will have the benefit of a "think-tank" or "internal" board to help in scanning the environment. This approach should lead to a more creative strategic control process. The eclectic multiple viewpoints of the team should lead to better judgments and more insightful interpretations. By maintaining a separation from the operating organization, the team should be more likely to provide a fresh view on critical changes complementing the insights of those executives who are most closely associated with the phenomenon in question. This results in a broader appreciation within the organization of critical environmental changes. Hopefully also, this might help prevent the dysfunctional effects from so-called group-think, which might result from the concurrence-seeking tendency that often exist among cohesive groups (Janis, 1972, 1982).

Role of Top Management

The role of the chief executive officer and top management in enhancing a meaningful evolution of the strategic control efforts consists of first understanding the importance of the overarching variables such as resource scarcity, information complexity, and information systems in the strategic control process, and second, effectively differentiating these variables across functions and organizational units so as to make the organization *simultaneously* responsive to changes in many different sectors and coordinated in both overall learning and responsiveness. Instrumental variables that can be manipulated to create this integration and differentiation include the structure of the organization, the value systems or culture, the reward and punishment systems, and finally, the internal information system. Figure 7.1 illustrates the interrelationships between the parts of an overall administrative system. Note when interpreting this figure that strategic control has been located in the middle not to signify a more critical importance than the other elements of the administrative system but merely to allow us to focus on the control dimension more squarely in this discussion.

Organizational structure is given a broader meaning than the way boxes are located in the organizational chart. It includes both the formal structure and the informal, emergent one—both permanent and temporary structures, both formal and informal processes. It is the overall mechanism in the organization that impacts the

Figure 7.1 Managing Strategic Change: The Role of the CEO

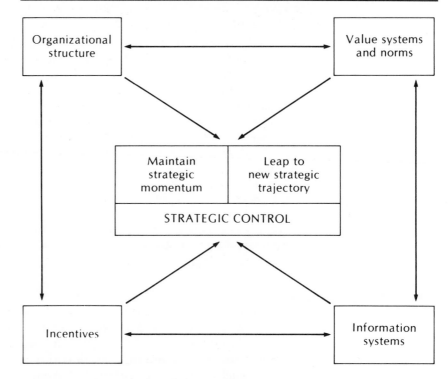

Adapted from the original teaching note by Richard F. Vancil and Peter Lorange, Strategic Planning Systems [*Englewood Cliffs, N.J.: Prentice-Hall, 1977*].

flow of information, the process of decision making, and the delineation of responsibilities.

The CEO must evolve a personal "map" of how the structure affects the organization's ability to monitor key environmental attributes. In constructing this map, the CEO can obtain relatively little help from theory or generalizations, since such maps are necessarily highly situation specific. They depend on the nature of the environment that the organization faces, on its niche within the environment, on its key success factors, and above all, on the strengths and weaknesses, values and beliefs of the people who inhabit the various boxes in the organizational chart. If the R&D manager in the company holds the strong belief that his or her job is pure research and is not willing to look into a problem unless it is esoteric enough to be at the cutting edge of theory, no amount of teams or task forces can make R&D more responsive to marketing and production needs.

The only solution to improve sensibility may be to replace the person rather than to create a system. Thus, in constructing the map, the CEO must identify the unique aspects of the organization, people, organizational areas, decision types, etc. that can significantly impact the strategic control process in a positive way, or, conversely, distort or paralyze the process.

The task of the CEO, with appropriate staff help, is to influence the addressing of the extent of integration and differentiation that should exist in different organizational subunits. In other words, the CEO must provide principal input indicating which parts of the organization that should be operating in a strategic leap mode and which parts should be managed for maintaining strategic momentum. As we have emphasized, whether to strive for strategic leaps or maintain strategic momentum depends not only on critical aspects of the environment, such as complexity, discontinuity, and malevolence, but also on the firm's strategy. Decisions about which subunits face a need for strategic leap are typically subjective and must therefore be exercised at the highest level where judgmental understanding of the overall strategy is expected to be most complete.

Subunits in a strategic leap situation should be provided with relatively more discretionary resources (i.e., strategic slack) and should also be relatively heavily integrated in management information and communication processes. More lateral relations must be created in those units through task forces and special teams. Roles and functions of individuals may be left relatively ambiguous and overlapping, and a degree of surplus resources must be made available with respect to management time and discretionary funds. The CEO may be expected to facilitate these changes. Even more important, the CEO might devote relatively more time to those subunits, to provide guidance regarding new strategic direction and to have an impact on the speed with which the new strategy is pursued.

Recall our example in Chapter 5 about the unhappy planner who was only comfortable operating within the strategic momentum context and who left the corporation as it moved to a wartime strategy. His failure to adjust was caused not only by the planner's inability to understand and adjust to the new strategic mode but also by the failure of top management to prepare him for the change. Investing time in such preparations is a vital task of top management in the overall process of operationalizing strategic control.

Much has recently been written about the importance of organizational values and culture, the second instrumental variable in the scheme suggested in Figure 7.1 (Schwartz and Davis 1981; Deal and Kennedy 1982). One fact that should be heavily emphasized from these discussions, and which often tends to be forgotten, is that an organizational culture—any culture—is never an unmixed blessing. A bureaucratic culture has its strengths and drawbacks, just as an organic culture has its advantages and disadvantages. A culture that is most effective in situations in which the task is to maintain strategic momentum is often a severe liability in situations calling for strategic leaps and vice versa. A respected American CEO described one firm's chaotic moves in the personal computer market as follows: "Hewlett-Packard has shown an uncanny knack of snatching defeat from the very jaws of victory." According to his analysis, precisely the same culture that made it an excellent company in its other business rendered it inadequate in the personal computer business.

The CEO must thus have a sufficient understanding of the cultures that exist in the organization and must identify the advantages and disadvantages this creates for the various organizational subunits facing different environmental conditions. We do not suggest that the CEO can change or create culture instantly, but an understanding of the different effects of the culture on different parts of the organization can help the CEO to make more salient the problems of adjustment and response that may arise and to establish adequate precautions needed to cope with them. An example that may be taken to illustrate such action is IBM's decision to completely segregate its personal computer business from the rest of its activities, at least during the early phases of this new business' life. The company may have recognized that the values that serve them so well in the mainframe market might impede success in the new venture. The creation of a separate subunit with explicit internal understanding of the differences that are required for succeeding in this different context may have been a key factor that allowed IBM to achieve outstanding success in the business.

The behavioral implications of incentive systems and, in particular, their effect on the control process have been discussed in the planning and control literature (Lorange and Vancil 1977; Anthony and Dearden 1980). However, the discussions have mostly assumed a maintenance of strategic scenario. The possibility of a shift to a scenario that involves strategic leaps opens up entirely new dimensions of such behavioral implications, which has important consequences for the process of strategic control.

Most incentive systems are based on performance measured by specific output variables: sales, profits, returns, market share, and so on. Such measures are typically appropriate during conditions of maintaining strategic momentum. However, in strategic leap situations, means rather than ends may become more important for control, and incentives based on behavior rather than on output measures may be more appropriate. This issue relates to our discussion in Chapter four of the different control mechanisms available to a firm. The work of Prahalad and Doz (1981) is particularly relevant in this context, suggesting a taxonomy of data management, manager management, and conflict resolution mechanisms as alternative ways for exercising control in complex organizations. In practice, firms may use a complex array of mechanisms, selecting components from all the three categories, but data management mechanisms may typically become relatively more appropriate in situations of maintaining strategic momentum, while the other two may assume relatively greater importance in strategic leap situations.

One excellent example of changing incentive systems to improve strategic control is Philips under the leadership of its CEO, Dr. Wisse Dekker. Facing, on the one hand, a long history and tradition of strong subsidiary autonomy that severely impeded exploitation of global economies of scale and scope, and on the other, an onslaught from Japanese competitors that made exploitation of those economies essential for survival, Dr. Dekker is reported to have substantially changed the incentive system in Philips to make the need for change more salient. The result was that a stronger sense of urgency may have returned to the company: "I wouldn't say there was no urgency around here before," says Dr. Dekker, "but it has developed greatly" (*International Management*, November 1982).

Finally, until the recent past, the top management of a firm has tended to have relatively little to do with the direct design configuration decisions regarding the information systems of the organization. The general perception has been that information systems were specialized functions best left to experts. Gradually, however, as the broader behavioral implications of information systems have become better understood, it seems to become clear that top managers must play a greater role in the design of those systems—not necessarily in a technical sense but certainly in a conceptual way. Already CEOs "have gone on line" in many major U.S. multinationals (Rockart and Treacy 1982).

Although we believe that a central role of top management in the strategic control process lies in influencing the context of control through organizational structure, culture, incentive, and information systems, their responsibilities do not end there. They must also be involved with the strategic control process in a more operative and functional way.

First, top management must itself be proactive in identifying critical environmental issues and in provoking discussions of them. They should articulate their view of environmental developments in terms of critical success factors. They also have to be sure that attention is paid to environmental scanning throughout the organization. The identification of critical environmental success factor is, after all, largely a function of top management's vision and insights. After extensive periods of maintaining current strategic momentum, top management may all too easily lose sight of this fact and allow their line managers to assume the sole responsibility for articulating critical success factors, thereby depriving the organization of the benefit of top management's insight and vision. These comments have been phrased in terms of a CEO who has been "lulled to sleep" by a continuing sense of business as usual. The same comments apply equally well to boards of directors. At the organization level, the efficiency of the capitalistic marketplace will ensure that only the awake survive. On a global basis, the risk is present that whole industries will not wake up until it is too late, thus permanently damaging the country involved.

Top management should also provide sufficient feedback regarding its approach to critical environmental developments. This may involve such actions as attempting to accelerate or delay the activities of the firm in light of environmental expected upturns or downturns, or implementing major shifts in strategy due to reassessment of the attractiveness of particular strategies, the risk dimensions of certain countries, and so on. The organization must understand top management's view of critical environmental issues in such strategic decision-making circumstances, and top management must share how they see their impacts on the overall portfolio strategy. Without such shared understanding, the rest of the organization may have a hard time responding appropriately to the information derived from environmental scanning and interpreting impacts on business or portfolio strategy that might result.

In general, the CEO must keep a creative pressure on the organization by being active in environmental scanning and by challenging the rest of the organization to be continually sensitive to critical success factors in relation to their individual environmental scanning and their interpretation of this information as part of their strategic control.

Another set of issues for managing the strategic control process relates to maintaining organizational realism as part of the environmental scanning process. A particular strategy will always have several critical success factors. Above all, the essence of strategic management is to be sensitive to the timing of particular decisions so as to better take advantage of an opportunity when it arises. Environmental scanning and strategic control must be focused on identifying critical bottlenecks that may impede the strategy or on developments that might open up an opportunity. Therefore, it is important that blockages of scanning be addressed. Especially when dealing with critical bottleneck issues, strategic control information must not be blocked.

Thus, an evolving strategic control system must build up a sensitivity to what is urgent. It must assist in the resolution of such urgent issues in terms of explicit decisions. The strategic control process should play a major role in shaping the agenda, in delineating the key issues for the organization. Such relevance and issue orientation are critical for strategic control. Unless the process evolves in this direction over time, and unless the members of the organization perceive that such an issue-oriented evolution is taking place, the likelihood that the strategic control process will become degenerative and excessively bureaucratic is exceedingly great.

Formats for strategic control must be relevant to the particular context at hand. Control processes often tend to become too paper oriented, often painfully laborious for executives to follow. A highly bureaucratic flavor may often characterize such control processes. It is important that strategic control is managed over time in terms of keeping formats in focus. Less central issues should be dropped, and formats should be flexible enough so that they are seen as relevant in different strategic contexts. Strategic control forms and reports should focus on the synthesis of what is critical, delegating background information to appendices or to computer bases. The format of the strategic control process must thus be managed so that it fits a particular context at hand, changing the format of the control process, the focus for what is to be controlled over time, reconstituting the strategic control teams, and so on. Managing the format for strategic control can thus be an important indirect way for management to ensure the implementation of strategic control. Although this task should be shared among several executives, the top management and the controller are likely to be key in interacting to cope with these issues. In the next section, we elaborate further on the roles of the controller.

ROLES OF THE MODERN CONTROLLER

The role of the modern controller as a key player in the strategic control process is critical. We delineate this role pattern in three major dimensions: the role as a catalyst (i.e., as a custodian of the management systems and thus a manager of the context within which strategic decisions are being made); the role as an analyst and thus the ability to contribute to the in-depth understanding of critical strategic phenomena, such as identifying and interpreting key environmental variables; and the role as a strategist, taking part in upper management's evaluation of various strategic signals and attempting to synthesize the meaning of all these signals into the proper strategic decisions and actions (Ackerman 1977). As we can infer, the role of the modern controller is likely to be multidimensional. The controller is a demanding executive position, close to the top of the organization and, in many ways, spanning the closeness to line management and the typical staff considerations of making management processes work.

The Strategic Controller as a Catalyst

The design of the strategic control system regulates the pattern of interaction and iteration among the line executives. As such, the strategic controller has a direct impact on the nature of this interaction process. The controller can influence who is talking to whom, about what, during which periods of time. This means that the strategic controller will have a major indirect impact on the nature of the strategic control process, via impacting this pattern of interaction in the process. The controller will have to be concerned about consistency in format, communication of time schedules, meeting schedules, and so on. He or she will also have to review the various sets of reported control information for consistency and synthesize it for more convenient use by line management. Finally, the controller will have to contribute to the modification of formats for control processes over time so that the control processes are internally consistent with each other and evolve in such a way that they support particular strategic realities at a given point in time. For instance, a particular business may evolve from a relatively new phase encompassing heavy growth to a more mature phase of a flattening out of growth. This would tend to be accompanied by a shift in critical success factors, from more environmental adaptation-oriented factors that would typically be concerned with how to capture the various types of customer segments with the appropriate types of products, toward a focus on more efficiency-oriented critical success factors such as ensuring satisfactory cost levels via economies of scale, standardization of product, controlling raw material supplies via vertical integration, and so on. A critical task is that the strategic controller facilitates the accompanying evolution of the strategic control system so that key success factors are allowed to be refocused according to changes in such strategic needs.

The Strategic Controller as an Analyst

As pointed out in Chapters 2 and 4 in particular, strategic control involves relatively more emphasis on the understanding of underlying phenomena and the delineation of theories of learining than what we have customarily been used to in traditional control. Thus, the strategic controller will have to try to understand why certain critical success factors should be chosen and what drives the various phenomena that these critical success factors represent. Therefore, the strategic controller must be broadly familiar with a wide number of underlying disciplines, such as economics, political science, sociology, and so on, he must be able to evolve the in-depth grounding of the strategic control system is such environmental-based "meta" theories. As we discussed in Chapter 5, on undertaking strategic leap control, the strategic controller must be able to carry out a number of ad hoc analyses over time, emphasizing a number of alternative analytical modes that require a diversity of analytical skills.

With strategic control information, therefore,, a more multidimensional analysis than classical performance deviation analysis is required. This demands an involved review of how to interpret a multitude of signals and to incorporate them into a sythesis and an analysis.

The Strategic Controller as a Strategist

Modern strategic control draws together a wide number of different phenomena. The strategic controller must be positioned in the top echelon of the organization in order to carry out the function of liaison with senior management on what these phenomena mean. He must be part of the strategic decision-making team in order to interpret what is going on. Decision making cannot be made without good understanding of the underlying assumptions upon which the control signals are based. The strategic controller will have to supply these types of insights to the decision-making team.

One might perceive a potential conflict of roles when a strategic controller is attempting to carry out all of these tasks. On the one hand, the controller is supposed to be the custodian of the system (i.e., the provider of the rules of the game for strategic control). On the other hand, the controller is also supposed to be part of the actual decision-making process that results as a function of the strategic control activities (i.e., is also asked to play the game). Can one person be a credible player when this person simultaneously controls the rules? We do not have a good solution to this potential conflict of interest. We can only say that the strategic controller should be sensitive to it. The person who holds the strategic control position must have sufficient seniority and insight to be able to cope with this issue.

A related issue is whether the strategic controller can play the customary role of somewhat independently reporting to various outside stakeholder groups, such as the board of directors and the stock-holders at large. We have clearly advocated a strategic controller role that is much more involved than that of the classical controller. The question of independently reporting to outside stakeholder groups might therefore naturally be spearheaded by the controller, but, unless done with sensitivity, may become a potentially controversial one. Our recommendation is that the board of directors receive a strategic control report specifically tailored for their needs, derived from the strategic control activities of the firm as a whole but limited to reporting on critical strategic factors. Left to the board members is then interpreting these issues and asking the strategic controller for an interpretation. Thus, a more detailed report to the board of directors seems called for than what traditionally seems to be the case—one that goes beyond the limited financial-based reports that the boards typically receive.

SUMMARY

In this chapter, we have discussed various executive role dimensions as they impact the operation of strategic control. This discussion had a three-part focus. First, we emphasized the central roles that have to be played by management teams in implementing an effective strategic control process. This strategic control process is, by nature, a complex, multifaceted one. Success is largely dependent on integration of many different signals, viewpoints, and theories, all of which are partly relevant. Such tasks can be carried out only by executives working in teams, forming think tanks to deal with strategic control phenomena such as delineating the critical environmental success factors or coping with particular pieces of environmental scanning information. The need to have a management culture that allows such teams to form and be effective seems therefore critical to achieving effective strategic control. The need to guard against degenerative group think is also key in this respect.

The CEO and top management must also play critical roles in the operationalization of an effective strategic control system. These roles must focus on the need to sensitize, push, and stimulate the organization to stay alert to the environment and not to slack off into too much internal focus. Partly, too, the CEO's own inputs are important regarding how he sees critical environmental issues and how to cope with given environmental phenomena. Above all, we have argued that the CEO must communicate any personal views on these issues to the broader set of executives, as this may be relevant.

An aloof and withdrawn CEO in this respect will not enhance effective strategic control.

Finally, we have discussed the diverse set of roles of the strategic controller. These fall into three dimensions: one is to be the custodian and promoter of the formal strategic control system; one is to analyze and interpret control signals; and one is to take part in executive team discussions regarding what decision-making actions should be taken.

8

Information Technology and Strategic Control

INTRODUCTION

Information Technology (I.T.) is important in any discussion of strategic control for two reasons: Most obviously it is an enabling force that permits powerful strategic control systems to be implemented in organizations. This is possible as we appear to have passed through a cost with functionality threshold where things long promised by the technologists are now being delivered. To use a computer example, anyone who has tried using the "mouse" pointer with pictorial instruction such as is available on the Apple MacIntosh is made aware that a new era is indeed underway. Computers and "chips" are, of course, only one segment of information technology as it applies to strategic control. Telecommunications and networks are equally significant. Information Technology as a enabler means that the data and manipulation we need to support managerially useful information can now be obtained.

Beyond Information Technology as an enabler for effective strategic control we have the reality of IT as a creator of more turbulence for organization. That turbulence increases the need for effective strategic control. For example, the electronic network that connects AHS customers to its ordering distribution system requires not only different operational controls for the sales force—but also different strategic control on variables such as emerging patterns in customer buying behavior.

The concept of strategic control as we have presented it in this book is not viable from a practical standpoint unless one can put in place low-cost, effective information systems. Such systems have to provide qualitative and quantitative data to the managers involved in time to be useful. Until recently, the only way to do this, at least in major organizations, was to rely on batch-processing computer-based information systems. Such MIS's were often based on the transaction-processing data base and were not unusually under the aegis of the controller.

Both the enabling and turbulence effects of IT are important at this point in time because the rate of change in the underlying technologies has been remarkably strong for the past 15 years and all the evidence (Dertouzos 1979) points to that continuing for at least the next ten years. We would argue that we have passed across a threshold (for example the ubiquitous nature of the personal computer) in the low cost and functionality of computers and in the emergence of powerful telecommunications networks.

Information technology is becoming less costly and more powerful with each passing year. Estimates of this change range from a low of 20 percent to a high of 30 percent each year for the next decade (1980–1990). Although this rate of change is genei .lly known, its implications are interesting. For example, Benjamin (1982) did a study in 1979 in which he derived the following data for his organization, the Xerox Corporation:

	1980	1990
Power	4.5 MIPS	4.5 MIPS
Cost (purchase price)	$4.5 million	$200,000–$400,000
People	210	4–8

Benjamin's study examined the cost of the large mainframe computer that Xerox had bought in 1980 for approximately $4.5 million. This computer had a power as measured by its hardware capacity of 4.5 million instructions per second (MIPS). This is, to an extent, an arbitrary measure of hardware power. It is also possible to use delivered power to users, as measured by solutions generated, but the final results would roughly be the same. In 1980 Xerox was able to hire 210 people for that $4.5 million. These people were high-level clerical or entry-level manager types. By 1990, at a change in cost of roughly 20 percent per year, a 4.5 MIP computer (that is, leaving the computer power constant) will cost in the neighborhood of $300,000. For that amount of money, 6 people can be hired, given the rate of inflation of people costs and the shifting mix of skills available.

The implications of Benjamin's study were not that organizations would shrink from 210 people to 6 people; from a social responsibility standpoint alone, this implication is clearly nonsensical. What is clear from the study, however, is that management has a challenge: to balance the absolute level of spending the organization invests in either computer power or people or in some combination of the two to make the organization as effective as possible in light of business changes. In essense, the challenge for the organization is to manage the trade-off between power, people, and dollars in such a way as to create the maximum value for the organization's stakeholders. One significant place to make such a choice is in the area of investing in systems for strategic control.

We look now at current technological trends to provide a better sense of the rate and nature of the change that is under way. In the second half of the chapter, we examine the implications of these trends for strategic control.

TECHNOLOGICAL TRENDS

Considerable change has taken place in technology since the first use of computers in business in the late 1950s. In the beginning, as computers were applied to organizational applications, the field was known as data processing and was primarily concerned with the automation of routine, manual clerical operations such as printing paychecks. In its next phase, the application of computers was labeled the MIS (management information systems) field, and the term captured the concept of using computers in business organizations to help management run their organizations.

Although DP and MIS once captured the concept of computers applied to organizations, this is no longer true. The computer industry has undergone significant changes and will undergo considerably more. The basic outlines of these changes are clear. On the one hand, we have a convergence of computers and communications forming a new combined field, and on the other hand, we have the miniaturization of computer chips. The combined result is often called I.T. (information technology). More than an evolution, it is resulting in the remaking of industries and the reshaping of corporations. These two forces of convergence and miniaturization are given real significance as a result of their spin-off effects in the fields of robotics with vision and intelligent workstations for managers and other professionals such as architects, engineers, and designers. In addition we have the digitalization of communications networks that will result in a soon-to-be-realized explosion of value-added networks (VANs). One example of such a VAN is the homebanking experiments being run by Chemical Bank of New York. This experiment will inevitably require a strategic control system to monitor and learn from this new strategic thrust. At the same time it is creating turbulence for the bank's competitors whose strategic control systems should have picked up on monitoring their moves.

Underlying these trends are four basic components: hardware, software, data bases, and communications.

Hardware

Although the classical, linear architecture still dominates hardware design, dramatic improvements in cost, performance, and size promote the emergence of powerful personal workstations and extend the capabilities of large mainframes. A number of technological advances underlie these trends, most notably improvements in chip-making technology promoting miniaturization and allowing the use of new materials (such as gallium arsenide) that are faster than silicon, and progress in circuit design primarily due to the use of increasingly sophisticated CAD (computer-aided design) systems, making possible new degrees of complexity and miniaturization. While further improvements in size and cost are to come, other forms of technology are even more powerful. For example, a whole set of possibilities are based on moving from electricity to light as a driving mechanism in parts of computers. Working prototypes of laser-based switches with phento-second speeds (10^{-14}) are now being used in laboratories.

Impressive as these developments are, they pale into insignificance in relation to the potential that exists in the parallel architecture machines. When research breaks open the "contention" issue inherent in multiple machines working on the same user problem, we will then have a whole new world of power opened up for use. This will be the kind of power that permits artificial intelligence and expert systems to be exploited by organizations. These two technologies are particularly suited for strategic control as they utilize human judgement and heuristics. Such concepts and tools lie at the heart of strategic control.

Storage is the other basic hardware component, and it, too, is undergoing considerable change in both an evolutionary and a revolutionary way. The evolutionary change will continue to yield 10 to 20 percent improvements per year through the use of tighter packing of molecules, better storage media, and so forth. The more revolutionary changes are gained through the use of new media, such as lasers and optical storage. These changes have already resulted in some clever applications of video disks and are a sufficiently different form of storage that they offer great potential for simultaneous, inexpensive, compact storage of voice, pictures, text, and numbers.

Such qualitative information is singularly appropriate for the multiple dimensions of strategic control.

Electronic technology offers a variety of productivity tools other than computers. Robotics are talked of frequently, although it is not often realized is how primitive our existing robots are. However, the potential that is now just visible in the use of robots with early vision systems and hands that can move in six axes offers a glimpse of what will be possible in the future. Similarly, professional workstations with powerful graphics and touch-sensitive screens, as well as the developments in voice input and output, give us an indication that we have scarcely scratched the surface of how we can support professionals in their daily work.

We have not yet seen low-cost, wide-band-width communications systems become widely available in the marketplace. Such systems will eventually be available at low cost. When this happens, we can expect to see the use of such things as video conferencing with life-size screens, full color, and full motion. This availability and use will have a profound effect on how and where we work, and how we should best organize ourselves in companies to do this work. Along with these changes will have to be changes in the strategic, tactical, and operations control systems. We glimpse this now as we watch architects or aircraft designers work at their professional workstations and create dynamic designs that can be manipulated, tested, and shared with workers, and then passed on to the next stage in the process without paper or clerical support of any kind.

Software

Software has now become the single largest cost of using computers. As languages increased in power and ease of use, training programmers became easier. This was partially offset by an increase in the size and complexity of the programs written. Improvements in programming languages turned out to be self-limiting, because the problem of understanding and the ability to modify problems over time to reflect changes are limiting factors to productivity. After we began to plateau in the improvements gained from increasingly better languages, a lot of use was made of applications packages such as prewritten accounts payable or accounts receivable systems. After awhile, we managed to come up with much of the standard widely used business applications, and the only ones that were left were the ones that had to be modified or that were unique to begin with. Thus, the latest trend that is visible is the provision of tools such as VisiCalc and other spreadsheet packages. These tools can become highly sophisticated, such as Express, the powerful modeling language developed by MDS (Horwich 1985).

Tools, such as VisiCalc and Express, in the hands of end users are now beginning to be matched by tools in the hands of information technology professionals. Professional workstations such as Intech's "Analyst's workbench" (*PC* Week 1984) provide an opportunity for the user to work dynamically with a pictorial view of the problem, such as a flow diagram. This diagram can then be manipulated to see if it produces the right results and works in the right way. Once that basic structure is correct, moving automatically to a working code is then possible. This step removes the programmer altogether and allows the analyst to be much more productive. It also opens up the possibility of end users eventually constructing programs that provide answers useful to their jobs.

In short, these trends in software point toward end users being able to use information technology in ways that enhance their jobs. At the same time, information technology professionals are being given the tools that will permit them to deal with the enormous complexity of real-time business problems and the vast networks of independent users that are part of today's business organizations.

To be effective, strategic control must be tailored to the managers and situations that actually exist. Such tailoring is most effective when it fits closely with the style and needs of the executive. Such a fit is best crafted either by the manager directly or with extremely close involvement of the manager. With the primitive tools we have had available until now, not surprising is that I.T. has been more of a hindrance than a help to the construction of effective control systems. The new generation of software tools offers hope for change.

Data Bases

Data is the fuel that keeps the engine of corporate information technology going. Thus, information management in general, and the design of data-base systems in particular, have become areas of real importance. Since the late sixties, organizations have tended to amass large amounts of data, usually a side product of traditional data processing systems, such as computerized budgeting, accounting, and transaction-processing systems. Data typically resided in a number of data bases, organized around hierarchical data models, each serving a particular application area. As these data bases kept growing, problems of incompatibility, inconsistency, and lack of accessibility proliferated, resulting in duplication of effort and inhibiting sharing of information.

The widespread solution was to move to more centralized data bases under the control of DBAs (data base administrators), who coordinated the use of data across different departments and maintained corporate directories. The development of "relational" data bases, which permit a more flexible organization of the data in nonhierarchical files, allow users to ask personally relevant questions independently of the way the data is physically stored in the computer files. Although this development alleviated some of the previous problems, several organizations have seen these centralized data bases grow to the extent that performance, maintenance, accesibility, and security problems have become difficult to contain. As a result, information management today represents a major problem inhibiting the effective use of information technology, but is also a major opportunity for those organizations that will face it successfully.

There are four major areas, in which current and future advances will affect the way corporate information is managed and utilized: data availability, data management, hardware and software architectures, and the design of relevant tools and human interfaces. Larger amounts of better-quality data are becoming available because of three underlying factors: improved data capture, vertical information integration, and external data bases. New operating procedures, such as the use of automated inventory management systems, and new types of technology, such as the use of optical scanners and UPC (universal product code) symbols, greatly improve the availability of data about many organizational functions. The development of electronic links between organizations and their suppliers or customers has been pioneered in well-publicized cases such as American Hospital Supply or the auto manufacturers, and will eventually result in the emergence of electronic marketplaces and the availability of a wealth of related data. Effective strategic control inevitably means having available a wide variety of different types of information from both inside and outside the organization. It is only recently that the advances in database software have offered cost-effective ways of employing such information as part of an effective strategic control system.

Independently from the data bases internal to specific organizations, an increasing number of external information providers exist, already in the range of several hundred. Thus, Dun and Bradstreet, Dow Jones, McGraw-Hill, and a host of others maintain data bases that are available to subscribers on a cost per use basis. These data bases cover every conceivable subject, are retrievable in whole or in part, and can be searched in powerful ways to find a relevant fact buried among an otherwise overwhelming mass of data.

Driven by the complexity of the data management problem and the trends in hardware and software evolution, data management appears to be taking the distributed route. Typical solutions will be based on departmental and subject-specific data bases, evolving around the specific types of data (e.g., marketing or production data) rather than on the particular applications using them. Assigning responsibility for the control and maintenance of these data bases will thus be easier, although an increased need for information sharing is likely to result. The next generation of data-base systems is expected to solve the problem of accessing, sharing, and preserving the integrity of these distributed data architectures while ensuring acceptable performance.

As far as hardware is concerned, a distinct trend is for corporate mainframes and departmental mini's to serve as data repositories, while the actual use and analysis of data will take place at individual PC-based workstations. This will allow mainframe-based software to focus on the efficient maintenance of data bases, which will often be physically distributed, while the PC-based software will provide an easy-to-use interface and a link to the mainframe departmental and other nodes on the organization's network. This link will be transparent to the user, who will not have to worry about the physical location of data nor whether the latter resides on the local workstation or on one or more machines on the corporate network. This transparency will be assisted by software providing integration between mainframe and PC software. Packages such as Cullinet's are the forerunners of this trend.

At the individual workstation level, data management software will provide the common basis that will allow the integration of different applications (such as analysis, word processing, and communications tools), a trend currently seen in the architecture of such systems as Lotus 1-2-3 or Symphony. In the near future, information management tools will be able to handle nonquantitative data, such as text, voice, image, and multimedia messages. Furthermore, dramatic improvements will occur in query languages, allowing nonsophisticated computer users to take full advantage of corporate data bases in creative ways. Today's state of the art already provides for highly interactive, example-oriented query languages (such as QBE, Query By Example), flexible query languages (such as on-line English), or even natural language queries in narrow subjects (such as Intellect). Future systems will greatly improve highly interactive, graphic, and less-restricted natural language requests for data, and will allow users to gradually build up these requests, thus zeroing in on their target rather than having to get it right the first time, as in today's systems. These changes significantly improve the quality of the strategic control systems potentially available (to the organization), for two reasons. The first has to do with the obvious benefits that occur from actually being able to get ready access to the relevant strategic control data. Until now this has typically not been realistically available. Increasingly it will be. The second reason that data-base changes will improve the quality of the strategic control system has to do with the ability of the person with the strategic control question being able to ask it directly and not having to go through a bewildering collection of programmers, analysts and remote main-frame computers.

Telecommunications

The newer technologies in telecommunications, beyond the "twisted pair" traditionally used for phone conversation, are microwave link-ages and fiber optics. Microwave is sometimes linked with satellites, which at once make cost independent of distance. Either or both of these technologies promise to reduce transmission cost, over the long run, by a considerable amount. An organization's view of tele-communications must now be expanded from internal narrow-band (i.e., traditional telex or telephone) communications to include the other two cells that will increasingly be in use.

The examples in each cell in Figure 8.1 are merely illustrative of some of the technologies that are now being used by leading-edge or-ganizations. Many of these examples should appear in more than one cell; for instance, computers can be linked by narrow-band linkages from suppliers' computers to the host computer as well as linked through broadband means. Nonetheless, the diagram provides one view of the expanding world of telecommunications that each organ-ization must deal with for its own purposes. The costs of communica-tions in each of these cells will drop continuously over the next de-cade, thus opening up new opportunities for organizations and for their related strategic control needs. For example, a face-to-face video conferencing set-up (in full color, full size and full motion) leads to opportunities for the kind of active informal discussions that lie at the heart of so much data collection for strategic control.

Figure 8.1   Categories of Communication

	Competitive Marketplace	Internal Operations
Significant Structural Change	Gannett—USA TODAY Merrill Lynch General Electric	Digital Equipment
Traditional Products & Processes	American Hospital Supply Bank of America Toyota	Xerox United Airlines

APPLICATIONS TO STRATEGIC CONTROL

These technological trends have obvious implications for strategic control and can be thought of as falling into two categories: the process of strategic control and the content of strategic control. Technology can provide tools both for the strategic controller and for the organizational process that is strategic control. We provide examples of this in the context of both momentum control and leap control. However, common to both is maintaining a live data base that is kept in computer-sensible form and can thus be modified, updated, and tested from any location at any time, no matter how remote. Texas Instruments provides a good example. In their case, they pride themselves on having no printed plan but rather an organic, living, strategic data base, which is accessed and sections of which perused and changed as needed.

Also common to both is the use of management support systems, namely decision support systems (DSS) and executive support systems (Rockart 1986). DSS are used by managers or groups of managers to reach a decision on semistructured problems—problems for which both facts and management intuition are needed. Clearly, many strategic control questions fall in this category. Such interactive use is sometimes designed to understand the variances—that is, the differences—between what was planned and what has occurred. To the extent that realistic strategic control depends a good deal on qualitative multidimensional information, interactive human-machine use as exemplified by DSS can be most helpful. In other instances, the differences do not need to be found, but rather a greater understanding of the causes of the differences is needed. In such cases, model building or model manipulation (or both) can be helpful—again, a good use of D.D.S. (See Morecroft 1984).

The use of executive support systems is of a more recent vintage and can also be thought of in two ways. One is the provision of multidimensional information, all of it in one room at one time with a variety of mixed media. This has been most visible in the literature on the military's use of strategic war rooms. The more common executive support center use is that of decision conferencing. Here, after receiving inputs from a group, the process moves on to reach mutual understanding of the problems and their possible solutions. In the case of strategic control, this would be mutual understanding of the differences that are involved or the range of causes that might be responsible. Phillips has done interesting work with chief executive officers and their direct reports on exactly this mode of decision making, and he reports considerable success in its use (Phillips 1985).

The other class of application of technology to strategic control is in the content of what is being controlled. Benjamin, et. al. 1984 described the four ways in which technology can be used to affect the strategic posture of a firm. They start by suggesting that an organization has two questions to address:

Can I use the technology to make a significant change in the way we are now doing business so my company can gain a competitive advantage?

Should we, as a company, concentrate on using I.T. to improve our approach to the marketplace? Or should we center our efforts on internal improvements in the way we currently carry out activities of the firm?

The first question is important because there exists today significant opportunities in some industries to utilize IT in order to deliver revolutionary new products—in effect, changing the industry—or to redefine completely the current approaches to manufacturing, purchasing, etc. This huge competitive "leap" should be a foremost concern of senior management; if it is not undertaken by one's own company, it is open to exploitation by others. Alternatively, if no such opportunity appears feasible, attention should turn to improving the current business through IT.

Moreover, there are two ways in which any business can be made substantially better: (1) improving the organization's impact in the marketplace; (2) improving key *internal operations*, thereby lowering costs or improving services. Our second question is meant to place emphasis on both ways. Most attention today focuses on using technology to improve the organization's impact in the marketplace. Most of the companies that we have seen, however, have significant opportunities to improve key international operations. Today's technology provides a myriad of ways to improve these operations (e.g., CAD/CAM for faster, better integrated manufacturing processes, electronic or voice mail for improved communications, etc.)

Taken together, the two questions suggest a four-cell strategic opportunities matrix, which is shown in Figure 8.1. We believe it presents a simple, but powerful, way of thinking about the use of IT. Each of the five companies presented below occupies a cell of this matrix. (Benjamin, et. al. 1984, 27)

The original article, from which we have taken Figure 8.1, contains an explanation of the role that I.T. played in each of the nine examples listed in the figure.

For example, with *USA Today*, a national newspaper is simultaneously created at seventeen geographically dispersed printing plant locations. This permits a central location for editorial and international coverage, which is sent by satellite to the seventeen locations, which in turn receive local coverage from their area through other communication linkages. The strategic control implications for such an organization is that it must have a major emphasis on monitoring the fit of the paper to the needs of their seventeen regions. Thus I.T. is having an impact on the kind of information needed for strategic control, as well as making it possible to collect and report such information.

A second example comes from the well-known American Hospital Supply (AHS) example. Their installation of a network linking their customers directly to AHS's computer permits customers to order directly without going through an order entry check or some other manual system. Such direct personal control over the entry process is appealing to customers. The implications for strategic control are two: monitoring of customer satisfaction and ensuring that the cost-to-serve numbers move constantly down the cost curve.

An example from a third cell in Figure 8.1 is that of Digital Equipment. As a pioneer in the application of expert systems, they were the first to put a configuration expert's judgment into a working system, which evaluates all orders before assembly and shipping. The strategic control variables in this sort of situation will center on measures of the success at institutionalizing the system and the success in building a new organizational team to capitalize on the system.

The fourth cell in Figure 8.1 contains an example from Xerox. In this case, Xerox created a fieldwork support system that provides field personnel with key data on equipment history, previous calls, and scheduling data. The strategic control variables here are measures of meeting productivity targets. Movement down this cost and quality experience curve is deemed critical to Xerox's success compared with that of their competitors.

In looking at strategic opportunities this way, the strategic control requirements can be seen to be different in each of the four cells. These requirements are summarized in Table 8.1.

Table 8.1   Strategic Control Implications of the Strategic Opportunities Framework

	Competitive Market	International Operations
Significant Structural Change (Discontinuity)	1. Scanning and positioning	2. Institutionalization and team building
Traditional Production Process (Extrapolation of Present)	3. Customer satisfaction Cost to serve	4. Meeting productivity targets

For expositional purposes, the arguments presented in Table 8.1 are drastically summarized. However, we can think of significant structural change as being synonymous with our use of discontinuous leap and traditional production process as matching our momentum category. In each of the cells in Table 8.1 are examples of items to be measured as part of the strategic control process. For example, in cell 3 customer satisfaction is likely to be a critical dimension that will require careful monitoring. Thus, measures must be derived to permit the organization to match the customer's evolving needs with the products or services and the prices that the organization offers.

LEAP CONTROL AND MOMENTUM CONTROL

Leap, or wartime, strategic control has at least two major opportunities for the use of information technology. The first of these opportunities involves the ability of the organization to scan its environment effectively. The external environment can be monitored either through the use of commercially available data bases, such as those provided by Dun and Bradstreet, or through government publications. Such data bases can be searched for major trends or patterns as they apply to the wide external environment in which an organization finds itself. The second form of scanning is that of competitive monitoring. In this case, a need exists to monitor particular corporations, either in the field with their salespeople and their customers or in the more formal sense of monitoring the reports filed with the Securities and Exchange Commission (SEC) or those that appear in the *Wall Street Journal* or the *New York Times*. If one knows who it is important to watch, it is surprising how much information can be found through the automatic monitoring of certain key companies and activities in publicly available information.

The second major use of technology for wartime strategic control involves the ability to rapidly assess the implications of certain moves. This so-called "what-if" ability allows one to look at the implications of a major acquisition or a major divestiture. One can specifically see what it might mean for the earnings per share or the debt-to-equity ratio or whatever else is regarded as critical in looking at the implications of making a major acquisition. This ability to assess the resources needed, and what the resulting financial position will be, is a powerful piece of input in looking at the implications of a possible strategic move. Nothing can supersede management judgment as to what does or does not make sense, but the ability to get the facts quickly and easily can make a difference at the margin to what one ends up doing.

Momentum control can be significantly affected by information technology, both for the process of control and for the content of control. In the former case, for example, a major U.S. bank for strategic reasons decided to decentralize their previously centralized management structure. This resulted in setting up 70 different profit centers, a number of which were strategic business units (SBU's). Also set up was a new reward and control system, which monitored the 70 different profit centers against the plans and targets that had been had set jointly by the profit centers and corporate management. As a result, many of these profit centers were asked to plan specifically for a series of strategic and tactical targets. Each of the 70 different profit centers was given a personal computer by the planning department and was asked to use the computer and its software to produce the profit center's annual plan. In each case, the profit center was required to return to the corporate planning department a floppy disk that contained information on the areas with which the central group was concerned. These individual 70 floppy disks were then transferred to a local minicomputer belonging to the planning department, and the data was then collated. After being checked and assessed for consistency, this data was put together in a form that could be reviewed by the planning department and ultimately by the chief executive officer.

Such a planning process and the degree of monitoring, evaluation, and discussion that resulted could not possibly have been done had it not been for the information technology available to the department. In this case, the technology was the widespread use of decentralized personal computers across the organization. In other organizations, the planning department has maintained, via terminals and a minicomputer, the strategic data that is required to assess the movement of the organization. Such creative use of information technology to monitor the process of planning is one way in which technology is turning out to be a powerful means of affecting the productivity of the planning effort.

Related to this is a more mundane but nonetheless real use of a new form of information technology. This use involves the communication levels between the relevant parties in an organization. Thus, a simple electronic mail system can be of enormous benefit, permitting different parties inside a company to communicate with low effort, low cost, and low time as they try to sense and exploit opportunities in the external environment. Although electronic mail systems no longer seem unusual, they provide interesting opportunities to increase the effectiveness of an organization's strategic control system when they are deployed worldwide and are easily available to key members of the organization. Similarly, maintaining the strategic data base, which may contain a lot of qualitative information, is something that can be done more easily through the use of a flexible, easy-to-use, electronic input mechanism. For example, voice mail reports from key members of the sales team is one mechanism that at least one organization has found an effective way of collecting anecdotes about fast-breaking developments in the field.

A different class of peacetime use of information technology is its use in reducing physical slack in the organization. More rapid or more accurate information can often be used to make significant reductions in the level of inventory required by the organization or the amount of time it takes to respond to a customer request or to bill a customer for goods supplied. A slightly more elaborate version of the same thing is the attempt by organizations to significantly reduce the time from the development of a concept in an engineer's mind to the time that concept gets delivered to the marketplace in a working version. General Motors appears to be trying to reduce the new car development cycle time from five years to two years. Such an effort opens up a new activity that has to be monitored in the ways described earlier in this book. Such strategic control activity provides the learning that lets management assess the progress in one of its major strategic thrusts.

SUMMARY

We have presented the trends in hardware, software, data bases, and telecommunications, and have maintained that the changes under way are merely the beginning of the availability of a set of powerful tools that will affect the strategy, structure, people, and processes that make up a living organization. These powerful changes in Information Technology (I.T.) are in themselves driving changes in the organization as the examples in this chapter have illustrated. However, equally important is the fact that this new level of cost performance of I.T. is enabling organizations to adjust powerfully to the kinds of major external changes that we enumerated in Chapter 1. The era of global competition is not being driven by I.T. but I.T. does allow an organization to adapt itself to this new era. Nowhere is that more apparent than in the arena of strategic control.

These shifts affect the way strategic control is exercised in an organization, as the new I.T. tools can alter the management processes available to set, monitor, and implement control. However, the power of I.T. also alters the number and type of strategic options open to the firm, which in turn alters the kind of strategic control that is necessary.

These changes are relatively new (Rockart and Scott Morton 1984) and will require continuing observation and research before we can begin to make normative statements about how things should be done. Abundantly clear, however, is that this area of change is one to be closely watched.

9

Issues for the Future

When considering future directions for strategic control, a useful starting point to take is the integrated viewpoint that strategic control is part of the broader set of management systems and processes as outlined in Figure 7.1. We see from this figure that the strategic control system cannot be taken out of its functional context: the organizational strategy with which it should interact and from which it should be derived; the organization's prevailing value systems and norms; the information systems available; and the incentives managers have. Thus, the evolution of the strategic control system will to a large extent depend on the ability to evolve linkages with each of these outer systems. It makes little sense for the strategic control system to evolve if the organizational structure remains frozen. This imbalance will result in an increasingly larger inconsistency between the formal structure and the strategic control system. Similarly, it makes little sense for the strategic control system to evolve if the value system and norms of the firm remain out of line with the new strategic control system.

In considering the evolution of strategic control, a useful approach is seeing how each of the critical parts of the outer system might evolve. The evolution of the outer system will define some of the constraints for how fast useful strategic control can evolve. Before proceeding with this approach, however, let us make a disclaimer regarding how Figure 7.1 should be interpreted at this point. We have portrayed the control system at the center of the exhibit. This is done for graphic reasons, not to suggest that the strategic control system is neccessarily the most critical system. On

166

the contrary, we wish to stress that strategic control should be seen as one element of a larger set of managerial processes, issues, and systems. As such, strategic control is an integral part of a larger concept, not the dominant part of this system.

CONSTRAINTS ON THE FUTURE EVOLUTION OF STRATEGIC CONTROL

One set of constraints on the evolution of strategic control relates to the evolution of the formal organizational structure. The organizational structure is intended to secure the efficient execution of value-creating tasks within the firm. This calls for an efficient division of labor and for a pattern of delegation with clear responsibilities. Bottlenecks in the decision-making and implementation processes should be eliminated. Formal organizational structures will then be based on a determination of how best to execute the day-to-day operating tasks within the firm. Formal organizational structure is to a large extent shaped by operating task requirements. To some extent the formal organizational structure must also reflect the particular strategies at hand (Chandler 1962). For instance, extensive divisionalization is a manifestation of this strategic variety.

Nevertheless, the formal organizational structure cannot typically always be adjusted on an as-needed basis in response to strategic environmental changes. Such overly frequent adjustments might have major dysfunctional impacts on internal communication, patterns of interaction, and learning, and would thus be extremely expensive. The organizational structure can never be expected to totally reflect the evolving environmental conditions at all given points in time. Thus, strategic control might be hampered in its evolution by the fact that formal organizational structures might not sufficiently reflect current strategic realities, since they were established on the basis of past conditions and operating pressures.

One way to deal with this issue, as we have discussed in Chapters 4 and 7, is to make use of less formal task forces, think tank groups, and so on to form an overlying strategic structure. This arrangement implies that the organizational members regroup to better reflect strategic environmental realities when resetting strategic direction, and that they will benefit from this regrouping when back executing through the more formal operating organizational structure. Although this process is highly promising, it requires a strong sense of homogeneity regarding organizational norms and values. Specifically, it requires members of the organization to have a real commitment to the organization, to share a common sense of values regarding how they view the organization, to be willing to live with ambiguity, and to see a certain amount of chaos as normal. If, on the other hand, the culture and values call for a strong delineation of task responsibilities, with heavy emphasis on the virtue of everyone sticking to personal territory or turf, and emphasize a functional preeminence while de-emphasizing a cross-functional, eclectical interaction across formal organizational reporting boundaries, and so on, then evolving a modern strategic control approach would be difficult. Thus, organizational development efforts and interpersonal conflict resolution training might be utilized to soften this barrier to further development of strategic control. In many ways, this obstacle to strategic control is particularly difficult—one that takes constant work and time to ameliorate.

The incentives of individual managers will also play a role in determining how fast strategic control can be expected to evolve. As pointed out earlier, and as found by the research of Lorange and Murphy (1984), the willingness to emphasize the importance of strategy implementation is not likely to take precedence if, at the end of the year when push come to shove, the bottom-line short-term performance is still counted excessively heavily in performance reviews. An evolution of incentives that emphasize a contribution to the development and implementation of new strategies must therefore take place. Such an incentives-setting process should incorporate more subjective judgments and make more acknowledgment of executives' contributions to the development of concepts rather than measurable outputs only; more emphasis on executives' ability to handle changes in environmental circumstances (i.e., their ability to act meaningfully when environmental circumstances shift and to take advantage of these changes); more emphasis on executives' contributions to think tank strategic control group activities, and so on. Such an evolution of the incentive system is therefore another development that might precondition the evolution of strategic control processes.

A critical issue for making strategic control more effective may involve the linking of strategic control to executive compensation and incentives. The argument has been made that the executive compensation and incentive systems commonly in use in many U.S. corporations today tend to create too much of a short-term operating focus. Executives tend to be trapped in focusing on the bottom-line results of the particular responsibility centers that they are in charge of, making it difficult for them to spend their own time and resources on initiatives required to establish strategies with uncertain payoff sometime in the future. A critical issue, therefore, is that even though many strategic control signals may be seen and privately accepted as important by executives, they may still not be acted on because of their possible detraction from the bottom-line performance of the executive in the short run. This behavior may have the consequence that by failing to confront the strategic issues now, any problems might potentially be much worse in the future. Dealing with the strategic issues at a later stage may be much more difficult. Also, the executive in question may count on a hope that someone else may be in charge when the strategy goes sour at that point in the future. The delineation of incentive and Management by Objectives systems that properly encourage the nonevasive and timely coping with strategic control signals is therefore critical in achieving more effective strategic control.

The strategic control systems outlined in this book seem appropriate for such an approach. Being explicit about what the critical underlying environmental issues are that might affect a strategy, including the bottom line for which the executive is supposed to strive, may make it easier to analyze what fraction of the bottom-line performance variance is due to environmental changes versus what fraction of the variance is due to performance dimensions under direct control of the executive in question. Performance failures do typically only to a certain extent stem from negative forces in the environment. An executive may also be helped by positive developments in the environment. In this case he should not receive significant performance bonuses since his results may have been achieved without any tangible superior performance on the executive's part.

By engaging in explicit discussions on the impacts of critical environmental factors at early stages, and with broad involvement of the executives in question, top management can more easily assess the individual contributions of various managers to insightful scanning of critical environmental factors, reacting to these factors, and reaching a managerial consensus regarding what to do in future. Therefore it may be feasible develop more of a de facto assessment of an executive in terms of individual contribution to strategic change based on environmental assessments. These judgmental factors should be part of the Management by Objectives system and should have significant impacts on bonuses, promotions, discretionary leverage that an executive can build up, and so on.

A critical challenge for the future is to develop the executive reward and compensation systems in such a way that they are consistent with the strategic control approach. If such consistency does not exist, then one would expect difficulties in implementing effective strategic control.

Finally, the information systems evolution can be expected to have an important bearing on the evolution of strategic control, which we discussed extensively in Chapter 8. A particularly critical dimension of the evolution of information systems will relate to the recognition of the cognitive limitations of executives in interpreting information and, above all, in reconciling various pieces of complex information. One can expect that cognitive limitations to decision making will play an increasingly important role in management information systems' evolution. Increasingly, the challenge will be how to present complex, multidimensional, multi-attribute phenomena in such a way that they are interpretable by manager. The evolution of the cognitive limitation and expansion dimensions of management information systems is likely to be another critical determinant for the way strategic control will evolve.

EMERGING ISSUES

The management of change is an area that still requires emphasis. What is known is not sufficiently well internalized and exploited by organizations, and research remains to be done in the field. Change is a social problem, and any social problem is relatively intractable. In part, we are seeking a mind-set change—a change that will allow us to keep the best of our existing base of practice in strategic control and yet move on to make the adjustments that are required in the times in which we can be expected to live.

In particular, we stress that the management of change should be seen as a welcome opportunity—a normal activity to be embraced rather than a necessary evil. We have stated that turbulence and rapid change are good, and that strategic control is a critical way to take advantage of these rapidly emerging opportunities. However, we realize that considerable modification of organizational culture and personal mind-sets will be required to embrace this viewpoint and allow it to become one with which individuals and organizations are comfortable.

Education of management has always been difficult and is doubly hard in this case, because we have historically been rational and analytical in the area of control. However, we are convinced that creativity and lateral thinking are absolutely fundamental for strategic control, particularly in time of war. This calls for an ability to look at the strategic control process as a learning process. A need will exist for better-educated executives who are aware that environmental signals can give them additional inputs and a better understanding of the true nature of the environment, so that their strategies can be updated accordingly. This calls for expertise from a number of eclectic disciplines and teams of executives who can share ideas and learn from environmental factors. High-powered, curious teams of executives with different backgrounds and experiences are therefore needed.

Education and understanding of change will not begin to take hold in the organization until the motivational structures and incentive schemes make it in the interests of management to pay attention to these issues. Getting the motivation right is partly a question of senior management leadership but is also a question of having the right incentive schemes and providing the right vision to the organization.

The problem for organizations is learning to cope with excessive change, both within the organization and in the environment in which the organization lives. Too much change requires that the organization focus on those few things that are most critical. If strategic control were the only task, an organization could readily put in place a new strategic control system. However, that is not all that is happening. Forms of competition, markets, and the economic environment are also changing, in addition to the personal lives of all members of the organization.

In this context, an instructive approach is to consider the state of classical control systems and cost accounting. In many organizations, these have frequently been poor for a complex set of reasons. Because the time has been one of peace, organizations have been able to muddle through while ignoring management control systems issues. If an organization has difficulty getting its classical control systems into shape, one can imagine how much more difficult it will be to implement an adequate strategic control system. One possible solution might be to put a strong executive in charge who recognizes the problem and can articulate the problem to the organization, and then use information technology as a vehicle to bring the new systems and procedures into being.

Another issue for the future concerns how to improve the timing decisions facing corporations—particularly, how to see the need for taking managerial actions earlier and how to build up an earlier commitment to the need for making a change rather than procrastinating over whether the environment is providing noisy signals that need firm ameliorating actions. The question of timing is perhaps the most critical issue of successful strategic management. To commit oneself prematurely to a new strategy can be both costly and, at the extreme, lead to the demise of the organization. Although this can be a problem, the more common problem seems to be that organizations commit to necessary changes too late. Rather than accepting that the environmental circumstances are changing, they often cling to false hopes that the good old days will come back and that a fundamental reorientation of its strategy is needless. To choose the right time for strategic change is the challenge. This issue is not new, but it seems to have become an even more critical issue for the future.

Strategic control processes should be able to contribute to better timing decisions in two ways. First, by doing a more explicit analysis of critical environmental changes, receiving early indications that something is happening in the environment is easier to attain. Having done a prior analysis of what the critical environmental issues are and how one's strategy might relate to these issues should make it easier to see what the significance of environmental changes are in the earlier stages and to react to them appropriately. Equally important, however, is the development of a culture in the corporation that attempts to face up to environmental scanning issues earlier and with more precision. A combination of better measurements and more explicit discussion of these measurements may make it more feasible to develop the necessary organizational confidence to face the fact that the environment is changing, and to develop earlier commitment to making organizational changes. A major issue for an organization is to be able to develop such confidence in the early interpretation of environmental signals and to develop a resolve to make changes at an earlier stage.

Again, although conceptually the strategic control processes developed in this book can contribute to such developments, a major challenge for the future is to reshape one's control culture to make such early decision making a reality.

One challenge that increasingly confronts corporations concerns how to react to environmental opportunities in a more creative, opportunistic way. This may increasingly involve the combination of various existing strategies into new ones or merging parts of existing strategy into new strategies. In other words, the fundamental challenge may be to react by managing across existing organizational entities such as divisions, countries, product lines, and so on rather than to change only a given business or country strategy in a more narrow, confined sense. Thus, organizational entities may have to face up to environmental challenges in a broader sense within the corporation. For a particular organizational entity to cope with environmental changes alone may no longer be feasible. Instead, drawing on a broad set of entities within the existing organization to deal with environmental change may be necessary. Increasingly, strategic control may imply an organizational ability to form coalitions internally for managing across the established organizational boundary lines (i.e., for establishing economies of scope within the organization). This means that strategic control activities, to a large extent, might have to be based on ad hoc management committees with representative from various organizational entities within the firm, and with early discussions of these environmental phenomena in a strategic think tank mode. By seeing the implications of such strategic changes at an early stage, it may be possible to rally the support of various established organizational entities within the firm so as to facilitate the proper mobilization of resources to meet new strategic challenges.

A difficult but still critical issue for the future is to lessen the reliance on established organizational entities when it comes to strategic control. In many strategic control activities that go on in practice, the case is unfortunately that the present organizational cubbyholes tend to dominate one's thinking and that facing up to strategic changes is difficult if they involve a redefinition of the boundary of the organizational entities facing the environmental issue. An organizational culture that attempts to build on the concept of a broader feeling of responsibility that goes beyond the formal operational, organizational authority it delineates is therefore critical and an important future challenge in making strategic control more effective.

An important dimension of strategic control is to understand when we are dealing with controlling the momentum of a given strategy (i.e., maintaining the particular strategic thrust) versus when we are controlling the leap toward a new strategy (i.e., setting the trajectory for a new strategic direction and the level of thrust for this direction). These two types of strategic control both involve, to a greater or lesser extent, the changing of organizational boundaries. Such change of organizational boundaries may mean that an emerging new strategy will have to be carried out by a different set of cooperating stakeholders, several of whom may be outside of the normal organizational subunits of the firm. Strategic control may require the development of cooperative strategies as a way of coping with environmental challenges. This means that the question of seeking out how to find allies, partners, other organizational entities that can be solicited as supporters, and so on is critical. The response to many strategic control challenges is thus not necessarily classical strategic warfare in the sense of applying more resources to remove a given competitor. Rather, it may be to delineate new coalitions of stakeholders so as to cope with emerging environmental issues in such a way that one's resources can be used for real forward leaps rather than in defending the status quo.

Examples of such emerging coalitions can be found in the high-technology industries—for instance, in the cooperation between such giants as AT&T and Philips in the worldwide telecommunications business. Rather than competing, they have decided to develop a joint approach to conquering the global market against Japanese, other European, and North American competitors. Thus, the boundaries for the organizational entities have been dramatically changed, now being much broader than would have been the case if Philips and AT&T would have reacted to environmental changes in the global competitive scene on their own. Another example of a probable need for redefining the organizational boundaries involves major environmental disasters such as the tragedy at Bhopal. Here, the need for broader cooperative effort between states, governments, corporations, victims' representatives, and others seems critical. For Union Carbide to react to this disaster within the traditional boundaries of its organization seems difficult.

The scope of this book has not been to provide fine-grained analysis of strategic control issues. We stress, however, that such analysis is needed. We particularly see it as worthwhile to develop a more realistic multidimensional cost-benefit analysis of when to expand and when to contract the scope of a given strategy. Such analysis will probably have both quantitative and qualitative dimensions. Such a framework would delineate when organizations should react to environmental challenges by building a broader, cross-organizational response (i.e., by building on the economies of scope). Conversely, it should also build on how the organization might strengthen its response by dismantling the economies of scope by adding more specific and narrow focus in its response reactions. Such fine-grained cost-benefit analysis seems to be beyond the comprehension of what we know how to do at this point in time. It definitely seems to be one of the challenges of the future that we need to address.

Perhaps the most fundamental shift in the evolution of control systems will be that top management will be expected to embrace strategic control systems as their own to a much larger extent than is currently the case. Today, management control is carried out by staff executives; the systems are relatively stable and well articulated and often heavily bureaucratized. The CEO can gain an important lever in personal efforts to manage the organization strategically by developing strategic control that is more line oriented, more flexible, and more directly impacted by the CEO. The strategic control system can offer the CEO an important opportunity to have an impact on the context within which strategic decisions are taken (i.e., to set the conditions within which executives can make better strategic decisions and implement them more effectively). Thus, by managing according to a strategic control philosophy the CEO can become a more effective coach for the organization in evolving good strategic management.

One critical issue for the future thus deals with how top managements of corporations will deal with the cognitive capacity limitations senior executives might experience in dealing with all of the various challenges the company confronts due to environmental turbulence, discontinuity, and change. The strategic control process can easily exacerbate the problem of the top management team and the CEO becoming a bottleneck when it comes to dealing with such critical environmental shifts and their impact on the firm's strategies. Such a centralized strategic control cannot work in practice, however, not least due to top management capacity constraints. One issue for the future, therefore, is to develop a more explicit framework of environmental scanning tasks and for delegating these scanning tasks among a larger number of executives within the corporation. These scanning tasks can be identified by means of the frameworks developed in this book, most importantly by building on how to monitor critical environmental success factors. The prior identification of such scanning tasks, coupled with a clear delineation of who is supposed to follow these scanning tasks, needs to be worked out. Additionally, one must delineate the pattern of who should get together to discuss changes in critical environmental assumptions. If the scanning should point out significant changes on a more reliable basis, which in turn might proactively trigger significant strategic shifts, this represents and important step to improving the capacity of the organization for strategic control. This might provide a broader involvement of executives in strategic control and a firmer commitment to strategic control issues throughout the organization.

Achieving a broader decentralized mode of strategic control and succeeding in making strategic control part of the key commitments of a large group of executives are major challenges. Organizations will have to keep experimenting with their management processes to make this happen in practice. This issue seems to be an important and critical agenda item for the future.

A major need exists for conceptual development and research on a wide range of topics needed to guide the direction and quality of the strategic control systems that are put in place. For example, issues as fundamental as thinking of organizations as interpretational systems have not been adequately explored and discussed.

The overall message of this book is therefore that strategic control must be seen as an integral part of strategic management for the future. We do not propose that strategic control should be made the focal point of future management practices. Rather, we have proposed that strategic control is a useful way of managing strategically and that it complements traditional managerial practices in a useful way. Above all, strategic control seems to offer evolutionary stimuli for strengthening strategic management in th years to come. The important message in this respect is that stra tegic control can speed up management's ability to develop adaptive organizations that can see environmental change and turbulence as opportunities rather than as threats, and which can build organizations that can evolve through learning rather than through disruptive breakups of established organizational forms (i.e., in a continuous fashion rather than through organizational earthquakes). As such, we consider strategic control a natural, essential part of strategic management for the future.

References

Abell, D. F., and J. S. Hammond. *Strategic Market Planning*. Englewood Cliffs, N.J.: Prentice-Hall, 1979.

Ackerman, R. W. "Role of the Corporate Planning Executive" in Lorange, P. and Vaneil, R. F., *Strategic Planning Systems*, Englewood Cliffs: Prentice-Hall, 1977.

Ackoff, R. L. *A Concept of Corporate Planning*. New York: Wiley, 1970.

Aquilar, F. J. *Scanning the Business Environment*. New York: McGraw-Hill, 1967.

———. "Managing the Quality of Strategic Thinking." Working paper, Harvard Business School, 1979.

Aldrich, H. E. *Organizations and Environment*. Englewood Cliffs, N.J.: Prentice-Hall, 1979.

Allison, G. T. *Essence of Decision: Explaining the Cuban Missile Crisis*. Boston, Little, Brown, 1971.

Andrews, K. R. *The Concept of Corporate Strategy*. Rev. ed. Homewood, Ill.: Irwin, 1980.

———. "Replaying the Board's Role in Formulating Strategy." *Harvard Business Review* (May–June 1981).

Ansoff, H. I. *Corporate Strategy: An Analytic Approach to Business Policy for Growth and Expansion*. New York: McGraw-Hill, 1965.

———., ed. *Business Strategy: Selected Readings*. Baltimore: Penguin, 1969.

———. "Managing Strategic Surprise by Response to Weak Signals." *California Management Review* (Winter 1975).

Anthony, R. N. *Planning and Control Systems: A Framework for Analysis*. Boston: Division of Research, Graduate School of Business Administration, Harvard University, 1965.

Anthony, R. N., and J. Dearden. *Management Control Systems*. Homewood, Ill.: Irwin, 1980.

Argyris, C., and D. A. Schon. *Organizational Learning*. Reading, Mass.: Addison-Wesley, 1981.

Athos, A. G., and R. T. Pascale. *The Art of Japanese Management*. New York: Simon & Schuster, 1981.

Bacharach, S. B., and E. J. Lawler. *Power and Politics in Organizations*. San Francisco: Jossey-Bass, 1980.

Barnard, C. I. *The Functions of the Executive*. Cambridge: Harvard University Press, 1938.

Bartlett, C. A. "Multinational Structural Evolution: The Changing Decision Environment in International Divisions." D.B.A. diss., Harvard Business School, 1979.

———. "Organization and Control of Global Enterprise: Influences, Characteristics, and Guidelines." Paper presented at the Colloquium on Competition in Global Industries, Harvard Business School, April 1984.

Baumol, W. J., J. C. Panzer, and R. D. Willig. *Contestable Markets and the Theory of Industry Structure*. New York: Harcourt Brace Jovanovich, 1982.

Baybrooke, D., and C. E. Lindbloom. *A Strategy of Decision*. New York: Free Press, 1963.

Beckhard, R. *Organization Development: Strategies and Models*. Reading, Mass.: Addison-Wesley, 1969.

———. Private exposition in Sloan School of Management, MIT, 1982.

Beckhard, R., and R. T. Harris. *Organizational Transitions: Managing Complex Change*. Reading, Mass.: Addison-Wesley, 1977.

Benjamin, R. I. "Information Technology in the 1990's: A Long Range Planning Scenario." *MIS Quarterly* 6 (2) (June 1982).

Benjamin, R. I., J. F. Rockart, M. S. Scott Morton, and J. Wyman. "Information Technology: A Strategic Opportunity." *Sloan Management Review* 25 (3) (Spring 1984).

Bennis, W. G., K. D. Benne, and R. Chin. *The Planning of Change*. 2d ed. New York: Holt, Rinehart & Winston, 1969.

Benson, L. T. "Impact of Information Technology on the Strategy-

Structure Relationship: A Case Study." Master's thesis, MIT, Sloan School of Management, Cambridge, May 1985.

Bourgeois, L. J. "The the Measurement of Organizational Slack." *Academy of Management Review* 6 (1) (1981).

Bower, J. H. *Managing the Resource Allocation Process: A Study of Corporate Planning and Investment.* Boston: Division of Research, Graduate School of Business Administration, Harvard University, 1970.

Bowman, E. H. "Epistemology, Corporate Strategy, and Academe." *Sloan Management Review* (Winter 1974).

Brown, J. K. "This Business of Issues: Coping with the Company's Environments." *Conference Board Report* 758 (1979).

―――. "Guidelines for Managing Corporate Issues Programs." *Conference Board Report* 795 (1981).

Burgelman, R. A. "A Model of the Interaction of Strategic Behavior, Corporate Context, and the Concept of Strategy." *Academy of Management Review* 8 (1) (1983).

―――. "Strategy-Making and Evolutionary Theory: Toward a Capability-Based Perspective." Research paper no. 755, Stanford University, June 1984.

Camillus, J. C., and D. K. Datta. "Designing Sensitive Systems: Integrating Strategic Planning and Issues Management." Paper presented at the annual conference of the Academy of Management, Boston, 1984.

Caves, R. E. *American Industry: Structure, Conduct, Performance.* Englewood Cliffs, N.J.: Prentice-Hall, 1964.

Chaffee, E. E. "Three Models of Strategy." *Academy of Management Review* (January 1985).

Chakravarthy, B. S. *Managing Coal: A Challenge in Adaptation.* Albany: State University of New York Press, 1981.

―――. "Adaptation: A Promising Metaphor for Strategic Management." *Academy of Management Review* 7 (1982).

Chakravarthy, B. S., and P. Lorange. "Managing Strategic Adaptation: Options in Administrative Systems Design." *Interfaces* 14 (1) (January–February 1984): 34–46.

Chandler, A. D., Jr. *Strategy and Structure: Chapters in the History of the Industrial Enterprise.* Cambridge: MIT Press, 1962.

Channon, D. F. *The Strategy and Structure of British Enterprise.* Boston: Division of Research, Graduate School of Business Administration, Harvard University, 1973.

Child, J. "Organizational Structure, Environment, and Performance: The Role of the Strategic Choice." *Sociology* 6 (1972).

Cleland, D. I. *Systems Analysis and Project Management.* 2d ed. New York: McGraw-Hill, 1975.

Cohen, M. D., J. G. March, and J. P. Olsen. "A Garbage Can Model of Organizational Choice." *Administrative Science Quarterly* 17 (1972).

Collings, R. F. "Scanning the Environment for Strategic Information." D.B.A. diss., Harvard Business School, 1968.

Cyert, R. M., and J. G. March. *A Behavioral Theory of the Firm.* Englewood Cliffs, N.J.: Prentice-Hall, 1963.

Cyert, R. M., H. A. Simon, and D. B. Trow. "Observation of a Business Decision." *Journal of Business* 29 (1956).

Daft, R. L., and K. E. Weick. "Toward a Model of Organizations as Interpretation Systems." *Academy of Management Review* 9 (1984).

Deal, T. E., and A. A. Kennedy. *Corporate Culture.* Reading, Mass.: Addison-Wesley, 1982.

Dearden, J. "Problems in Decentralized Profit Responsibility." *Harvard Business Review* (May–June 1960).

———. *Cost and Budget Analysis.* Englewood Cliffs, N.J.: Prentice-Hall, 1962.

Dertouzos, M. L., and J. Moses, eds. *The Computer Age: A Twenty-Year View.* Cambridge: MIT Press, 1979.

Dill, W. R. "Environment as an Influence on Managerial Autonomy." *Administrative Science Quarterly* 2 (1958).

Doz, Y., and C. K. Prahalad. "Headquarter Influence and Strategic Control in MNCs." *Sloan Management Review* 22 (4) (Fall 1981).

———. "Patterns of Strategic Control within Multinational Corporations." *Journal of International Business Studies* 15 (2) (Fall 1984).

Drucker, P. F. *The Age of Discontinuity: Guidelines to Our Changing Society.* New York: Harper & Row, 1969.

———. *Management: Tasks, Responsibilities, Practices.* New York: Harper & Row, 1974.

———. *Managing in Turbulent Times.* London: Heinemann, 1980.

Duncan, R. B. "Characteristics of Organizational Environments and Perceived Environmental Uncertainty." *Administrative Science Quarterly* 17 (1972).

Duncan, R., and A. Weiss. "Organizational Learning: Implications for Organizational Design." In *Research in Organizational Behavior*, vol. 1, edited by B. Staw. Greenwich: JAI Press, 1978.

Dutton, J. E., and R. B. Duncan. "The Influence of the Strategic Planning Process on Strategic Change." Paper presented at the annual conference of the Academy of Management, Boston, 1984.

Dyas, G. P., and H. T. Thanheiser. *The Emerging European Enterprise: Strategy and Structure in French and German Industry*. London: Macmillan, 1976.

Edmunds, S. W. "The Role of Future Studies in Business Strategic Planning." *Journal of Business Strategy* (Spring 1984).

Emery, F. E., and E. L. Trist. *Towards a Social Ecology*. Plenum Press, London, 1973.

EMI and the CT Scanner (A) and (B). ICCH 9-363-194/195. Harvard Business School cases, 1983.

Evans, J. S. "Strategic Flexibility in Business." SRI International Business Intelligence Program, report no. 678, December 1982.

Feldman, M. S., and J. G. March. "Information in Organizations as Signal and Symbol." *Administrative Science Quarterly* 26 (1981).

Forrester, J. W. *Principles of Systems*. Cambridge: MIT Press, 1981.

Fortune. "Oh Where, Oh Where Has My Little Dog Gone? Or My Cash Cow? Or My Star?" 2 November 1981, 148–54.

Galbraith, J. *Designing Complex Organizations*. Reading, Mass. Addison-Wesley, 1973.

Galbraith, J. R., and R. K. Kazanjian. *Strategy Implementation: The Role of Structure and Process*. 2d ed. St. Paul: West, 1986.

Goodman, P. S., and Associates. *Changes in Organizations*. San Francisco: Jossey-Bass, 1982.

Goodman, P. S., M. Bazerman, and E. Conlon. "Institutionalization of Planned Organizational Change." In *Research in Organizational Behavior*, vol. 2, edited by B. M. Staw and L. L. Cummings. Greenwich: JAI Press, 1979.

Goodman, P. S., and J. W. Dean, Jr. "Creating Long-Term Organizational Change." In *Change in Organizations*, edited by P. S. Goodman and Associates. San Francisco: Jossey-Bass, 1982.

Gordon, T. J., and O. Helmer. "Report on Long-Range Forecasting Study." Paper P-2982, Santa Monica: Rand Corporation, September 1964.

Gorry, G. A., and M. S. Scott Morton. "A Framework for Management Information Systems." *Sloan Management Review* 13 (1971).

Hambrick, D. "Some Tests of the Effectiveness and Functional Attributes of Miles and Snow's Strategic Types." *Academy of Management Journal* (1983).

Hambrick, D. C., and C. C. Snow. "A Contextual Model of Strategic Decision Making in Organizations." In *Academy of Management Proceedings,* edited by R. L. Taylor, J. J. O'Connell, R. A. Zawacki, and D. D. Warrick, 109–12, 1977.

Hamel, G., and C. K. Prahalad. "Managing Strategic Responsibility in the MNC." *Strategic Management Journal* 4 (1983).

Hannan, M., and J. Freeman. "The Population Ecology of Organizations." *American Journal of Sociology* 83 (1977).

Hax, A. C., and N. S. Majluf. *Strategic Management: Integrative Perspective.* Englewood Cliffs, N.J.: Prentice-Hall, 1984.

Hedberg, B. "How Organizations Learn and Unlearn." In *Handbook of Organizational Design,* edited by D. C. Nystrom and W. H. Starbuck. Oxford: Oxford University Press, 1981.

Hedberg, B.O.L.T., P. C. Nystrom, and W. H. Starbuck. "Camping on Seesaws: Prescriptions for a Self-designing Organization." *Administrative Science Quarterly* 21 (1976).

Henderson, B. D. *Henderson on Corporate Strategy.* Cambridge, Mass.: Abt Books, 1979.

Hofer, C. W., and D. Schendel. *Strategy Formulation: Analytical Concepts.* St. Paul: West, 1978.

Horngren, C. T. *Cost Accounting: A Managerial Emphasis.* 3d ed. Englewood Cliffs, N.J.: Prentice-Hall, 1972.

Hornstein, H. A., B. B. Bunker, W. W. Burke, M. Gindes, and R. J. Lewicki. *Social Intervention.* New York: Free Press, 1971.

Horowitt, E. "A New Language for Managers." *Business Computer Systems* (January 1985): 62.

Janis, I. L. *Victims of Groupthink,* Boston: Houghton Mifflin, 1972.

Janis, I. L. *Groupthink: Psychological Studies of Policy Decisions and Fiascos,* Boston: Houghton Mifflin, 1982.

Jarillo, J. C. "Entrepreneurship: A Conceptual Framework." Unpublished paper. Boston: Harvard Business School, November 1984.

Jefferson, J. M. "Economic Uncertainty and Decision Making." Paper presented at the annual meeting of the British Association for the Advancement of Science, September 1981.

Jerome, W. T. III, *Executive Control: The Catalyst,* New York: Wiley, 1961.

Jurkovich, R. "A Core Typology of Organizational Environments." *Administrative Science Quarterly* 19 (1974).

Kahn, R. L. "Conclusions: Critical Themes in the Study of Change." In *Change in Organizations*, edited by P. S. Goodman and Associates. San Francisco: Jossey-Bass, 1982.

Kanter, R. M. *The Change Masters*. New York: Simon & Schuster, 1983.

Keegan, W. J. "Scanning the International Business Environment: A Study of the Information Acquisition Process." D.B.A. diss., Harvard Business School, 1967.

Keen, P. G. W., and M. S. Scott Morton. *Decision Support Systems: An Organizational Perspective*. Reading, Mass.: Addison-Wesley, 1978.

Kiesler, S., and L. Sproull. "Managerial Response to Changing Environments: Perspectives on Problem Sensing from Social Cognition." *Administrative Science Quarterly* 27 (1982).

King, W. R. "Using Strategic Issue Analysis." *Long Range Planning* 15 (August 1982).

King, W. R., and D. I. Cleland. *Strategic Planning and Policy*. New York: Van Nostrand, 1978.

Klaassen, J. *Current Replacement Value Accounting in Western Europe*. Oklahoma State University Monograph, Oklahoma City, 1976.

Klein, H. E., and R. E. Linneman. "Environmental Assessment: An Internal Study of Corporate Practice." *Journal of Business Strategy* (Spring 1984).

Kogut, B. "Normative Observations on the International Value-Added Chain and Strategic Groups." Working paper no. WP-84-04, Reginald Jones Center, Wharton School, Philadelphia, February 1984.

Lawrence, P. R., and D. Dyer. *Renewing American Industry*. New York: Free Press. 1983.

Lawrence, P. R., and J. W. Lorsch. *Organization and Environment: Managing Differentiation and Integration*. Boston: Division of Research, Graduate School of Business Administration, Harvard University, 1967.

Leichtman, S., "Implementing Strategic Change at the Coca-Cola Company, 1980–1985", unpublished paper, The Sloan School of Management, MIT, 1985.

Lessard, D. R., ed. *International Financial Management: Theory and Applications*. Boston: Warren, Gorham & Lamont, 1979.

————. "Finance and Global Competition." Paper presented at the Colloquium on Competition in Global Industries, Harvard Business School, April 1984.

Lewin, K. *Field Theory in Social Science.* New York: Harper & Row, 1951.

————. "Group Decision and Social Change." In *Readings in Social Psychology,* rev. ed., edited by G. E. Swanson, T. N. Newcomb, and E. L. Hartley. New York: Holt, Rinehart & Winston, 1952.

Lindbloom, C. E. "The Science of Muddling Through." *Public Administration Review* 19 (1959).

Lippitt, R., J. Watson, and B. Westley. *The Dynamics of Planned Change.* New York: Harcourt Brace Jovanovich, 1958.

Little, Arthur D., Inc. *A System for Managing Diversity.* Cambridge, Mass.: Arthur D. Little, 1974.

Lodge, G. C. *The New American Ideology.* New York: Knopf, 1975.

Lorange, P. *Corporate Planning: An Executive Viewpoint.* Englewood Cliffs, N.J.: Prentice-Hall, 1980.

————. "Strategic Control: Some Issues in Making It Operationally More Useful." In *Competitive Strategic Management,* edited by R. Lamb. Englewood Cliffs, N.J.: Prentice-Hall, 1984.

Lorange, P., and D. Murphy. "Considerations in Implementing Strategic Control." *Journal of Business Strategy* 4 (4) (Spring 1984).

Lorange, P., and R. F. Vancil. *Strategic Planning Systems.* Englewood Cliffs, N.J.: Prentice-Hall, 1977.

MacMillan, I. C. "Seizing Competitive Initiative." *Journal of Business Strategy* 2 (4) (Spring 1982).

Marakon Associates. "The Role of Finance in Strategic Planning." Business Week Conference, New York, 1980.

March, J. G., and J. P. Olsen. *Ambiguity and Choice in Organizations.* Bergen, Norway: Universitetsforlaget, 1976.

March, J. G., and H. A. Simon. *Organizations.* New York: Wiley, 1958.

McCosh, A. M., and M. S. Scott Morton. *Management Decision Support System.* London: Macmillan, 1978.

Meyer, J. W., and B. Rowan. "Institutionalized Organizations: Formal Structure as Myth and Ceremony." *American Journal of Sociology* 83 (1977).

Miles, R. E., and C. C. Snow. *Organizational Strategy, Struture, and Process.* New York: McGraw-Hill, 1978.

Miles, R. E., C. C. Snow, and J. Pfeffer. "Organization-Environment: Concepts and Issues." *Industrial Relations* 13 (1974).

Miller, D., and P. H. Friesen. *Organizations: A Quantum View.* Englewood Cliffs, N.J.: Prentice-Hall, 1984.

Mintzberg, H. *The Nature of Managerial Work.* New York: Harper & Row, 1973.

———. "Patterns in Strategy Formulation." *Management Science* 24 (1978).

———. *Power in and Around Organizations.* Englewood Cliffs, N.J.: Prentice-Hall, 1983.

Montgomery, D. B., and C. B. Weinberg. "Toward Strategic Intelligence Systems." *Journal of Marketing* (Fall 1979).

Morecroft, J. D. W. "Strategy Support Models." *Strategic Management Journal* 5 (3) (1984): 215–29.

Morecroft, J. D. W., and M. Paich. "System Dynamics for the Design of Business Policy and Strategy." Working paper WP-1606-84, Sloan School of Management, MIT, October 1984.

Nadler, D. A. "Managing Organizational Change: An Integrative Perspective." *Journal of Applied Behavioral Science* 17 (1981).

Naisbitt, J. *Megatrends.* New York: Warner Books, 1982.

Naylor, T. H. *Corporate Planning Models.* Reading, Mass.: Addison-Wesley, 1979.

Pascale, R. T., and A. G. Athos. *The Art of Japanese Management: Applications for American Executives.* New York: Simon & Schuster, 1981.

Pavan, R. J. "The Strategy and Structure of Italian Enterprise." DBA thesis, Graduate School of Business Administration, Harvard University, 1972.

PC Week, September 25, 1984, Ziff-Dan's; New York, N.Y.

Peters, T. J., and R. H. Waterman, Jr. *In Search of Excellence: Lessons from America's Best Run Companies.* New York: Harper & Row, 1982.

Pettigrew, A. M. *The Politics of Organizational Decision Making.* London: Tavistock, 1973.

———. "Culture and Politics in Strategic Decision Making and Change." Paper presented to the Symposium on Strategic Decision Making in Complex Organizations, Columbia University, November 1983.

Pfeffer, J. *Organizational Design.* Arlington Heights, Ill.: AHM Publishing, 1978.

———. *Power in Organizations.* Marshfield, Mass.: Pitman, 1981.

———. *Organizations and Organization Theory.* Marshfield, Mass.: Pitman, 1982.

Pfeffer, J., and G. R. Salancik. *The External Control of Organizations: A Resources Dependence Perspective.* New York: Harper & Row, 1978.

Phillips, L. D. "Decision Support for Senior Executives." *Datamation* (Fall 1985).

Piore, M. J., and C. F. Sabel. *The Second Industrial Divide.* New York: Basic Books, 1984.

Porter, M. E. *Competitive Strategy.* New York: Free Press, 1980.

———. *Cases in Competitive Strategy.* New York: Free Press, 1983.

———. "Competition in Global Industries: A Conceptual Framework." Paper presented at the Colloquium on Competition in Global Industries, Harvard Business School, April 1984.

———. *Competitive Advantage.* New York: Free Press, 1985.

Pounds, W. F. "The Process of Problem Finding." Working paper 148–65, Sloan School Management, MIT, Cambridge, 1965.

Prahalad, C. K. "Strategic Choices in Diversified MNC's." *Harvard Business Review* 54 (4) (July–August 1976).

Quinn, J. B. *Strategies for Change: Logical Incrementalism.* Homewood, Ill.: Irwin, 1980.

Rappaport, A., ed. *Information for Decision Making: Quantitative and Behavioral Dimensions.* 2d ed. Englewood Cliffs, N.J.: Prentice-Hall, 1975.

———. "Selecting Strategies that Create Shareholder Value." *Harvard Business Review* 59 (3) (May–June 1981).

Reece, J. S., and W. R. Cool. "Measuring Investment Center Performance." *Harvard Business Review* (May–June 1978).

Rockart, J. "Chief Executives Define Their Own Data Needs." *Harvard Business Review* 57 (2) (March–April 1979).

Rockart, J. (ed.), *The Best of CISR,* Dow Jones-Irvin, New York, 1986.

Rockart, J. F., and M. S. Scott Morton. "Implications of Changes in Information Technology for Corporate Strategy." *Interfaces* 14 (1) (January–February 1984): 84–95.

Rockart, J. F., and M. E. Treacy. "The CEO Goes On-Line." *Harvard Business Review* 60 (1) (January–February 1982): 82–88.

Rostow, W. W. *The Stages of Economic Growth.* Cambridge: Cambridge University Press, 1960.

Rothschild, W. E. "How to Ensure the Continued Growth of Strategic Planning, *Journal of Business Strategy*, vol. 1, no. 1, 1980.

Rumelt, R. P. *Strategy, Structure, and Economic Performance*. Boston: Division of Research, Graduate School of Business Administration, Harvard University, 1974.

Salter, M. S., and W. A. Weinhold. *Diversification through Acquisition*. New York: Free Press, 1979.

Schein, E. H. *Process Consultation: Its Role in Organization Development*. Reading, Mass.: Addison-Wesley, 1969.

————. *Career Dynamics: Matching Individual and Organizational Needs*. Reading, Mass.: Addison-Wesley, 1978.

————. *Organizational Psychology*. 3d ed. Englewood Cliffs, N.J.: Prentice-Hall, 1980.

Schoeffler, S. R., R. D. Buzzell, and D. F. Heaney. "Impact of Strategic Planning on Profit Performance." *Harvard Business Review* (March–April 1974).

Schroder, H. M., M. J. Drive, and S. Streufert. *Human Information Processing*. New York: Holt, Rinehart & Winston, 1967.

Schwartz, H., and S. M. Davis. "Matching Corporate Culture and Business Strategy." *Organizational Dynamics* 10 (Summer 1981).

Selznick, P. *Leadership in Administration*. Evanston, Ill.: Row, Peterson, 1957.

Simon, H. A. *Administrative Behavior*. New York: Free Press, 1957.

Starbuck, W. H. "Organizations and Their Environments." In *Handbook of Industrial and Organizational Psychology*, edited by M. D. Dunnette. Chicago: Rand McNally, 1976.

Starbuck, W. H., and B.O.L.T. Hedberg. "Saving an Organization from a Stagnating Environment." In *Strategy + Structure = Performance*, edited by H. G. Thorelli. Bloomington: Indiana University Press, 1977.

Staw, B. M. "Counterforce to Change." In *Change in Organizations*, edited by P. S. Goodman and Associates. San Francisco: Jossey-Bass, 1982.

Steiner, G. A. *Strategic Planning: What Every Manager Must Know*. New York: Free Press, 1979.

Strategic Planning Associates, Inc. "Commentaries: Beyond the Portfolio." Washington, D. C.: Strategic Planning Associates, 1981.

————. "Strategy and Shareholder Value: The Value Curve." In *Competitive Strategic Management*, edited by R. B. Lamb. Englewood Cliffs, N.J.: Prentice-Hall, 1984.

Taylor, F. W. *The Principles of Scientific Management*. New York: Harper & Brothers, 1911.

Terpstra, V. *International Dimensions of Marketing*. Boston: Kent, 1982.

Terreberry, S. "The Evolution of Organizational Environments." *Administrative Science Quarterly* 12 (1968).

Thompson, J. D. *Organizations in Action: Social Science Bases of Administrative Theory*. New York: McGraw-Hill, 1967.

Toffler, A. *Future Shock*. New York: Random House, 1970.

Tosi, H., R. Aldag, and R. Storey. "On the Measurement of the Environmental Unvertainty Scale." *Administrative Science Quarterly* 17 (1972).

Vancil, R. F. "What Kind of Management Control Do You Need?" *Harvard Business Review* (March–April 1973).

————. *Implementing Strategy: The Role of Top Management*. Boston: Division of Research, Harvard Business School, 1982.

Vernon, R. *Sovereignty at Bay: The Multinational Spread of U.S. Enterprises*. New York: Basic Books, 1971.

Wack, P. A. "Earning to Design Planning Scenarios: The Experience of Royal Dutch Shell." Unpublished manuscript, Harvard Business School, March 1984.

Weber, M. *The Theory of Social and Economic Organizations*, translated by A. M. Henderson and T. Parsons. New York: Free Press, 1947.

Weick, K. E. *The Social Psychology of Organizing*. Reading, Mass.: Addison-Wesley, 1969.

Weiss, E. A. "How the Sun Company Assesses the Future Business Environment." Speech presented to the Public Affairs Council's Workshop on Forecasting and Managing Issues, May 1978.

Wells, J. "In Search of Synergy Strategies for Related Diversification." Thesis proposal, Harvard Business School, 1984.

Wilensky, H. L. *Organizational Intelligence*. New York: Basic Books, 1967.

Williamson, D. E. *The Economics of Discretionary Behavior*. Englewood Cliffs, N.J.: Prentice-Hall, 1964.

Wrigley, L. "Divisional Autonomy and Diversification." D.B.A. diss., Harvard Business School, 1970.

Zalesnik, A., and M. F. R. Kets de Vries. *Power and the Corporate Mind.* Boston: Houghton Mifflin, 1975.

Zucker, L. G. "The Role of Institutionalization in Cultural Persistence." *American Sociological Review* 42 (1977).

INDEX